DRAMA CLASSICS

The Drama Classics series aims to offer the world's greatest plays in affordable paperback editions for students, actors and theatregoers. The hallmarks of the series are accessible introductions, uncluttered texts and an overall theatrical perspective.

Given that readers may be encountering a particular play for the first time, the introduction seeks to fill in the theatrical/historical background and to outline the chief themes rather than concentrate on interpretational and textual analysis. Similarly the play-texts themselves are free of footnotes and other interpolations: instead there is an end-glossary of 'difficult' words and phrases.

The texts of the English-language plays in the series have been prepared taking full account of all existing scholarship. The foreign-language plays have been newly translated into a modern English that is both actable and accurate: many of the translators regularly have their work staged professionally.

Edited until his early death by Kenneth McLeish, the Drama Classics series continues with his aim of providing a first-class library of dramatic literature representing the best of world theatre.

Associate editors:
Professor Trevor R. Griffiths
Visiting Professor in Humanities, Universities of Exeter and Hertfordshire
Dr Colin Counsell
School of Humanities, Arts and Languages,
London Metropolitan University

DRAMA CLASSICS *the first hundred*

*The publishers welcome
suggestions for further titles*

DRAMA CLASSICS

AN IDEAL HUSBAND

by
Oscar Wilde

edited and with an introduction by
Laurie Wolf

NICK HERN BOOKS
London
www.nickhernbooks.co.uk

A Drama Classic

This edition of *An Ideal Husband* first published
in Great Britain as a paperback original in 1999
by Nick Hern Books Limited, 14 Larden Road, London W3 7ST

Reprinted 2001, 2005, 2010

Typeset by Country Setting, Kingsdown, Kent CT14 8ES
Printed and bound in Great Britain by Bookmarque,
Croydon, Surrey

A CIP catalogue record for this book is available from
the British Library

ISBN-13   978 1 85459 460 0

Introduction

Oscar Wilde (1854-1900)

Wilde was born in 1854, the second son of Sir William Charles
Kingsbury Wills Wilde, a doctor and writer and Lady Jane
Wilde, a poet and Irish Nationalist. He and his older brother
were boarders in the Portora School at Enniskillen, one of the
four Royal schools in Ireland. He left the school at sixteen
when he won a place at Trinity College, Dublin, to read
English and Classics; it was here that he first discovered
Swinburne, Rosetti, Whitman and Symonds – the artists and
writers who gave him his first clear insight into a world of
beauty and art. After completing his degree at Trinity, he won
a classical scholarship to study for a second undergraduate
degree at Oxford.

Throughout his life, Oscar Wilde made it his task to improve
on nature's creations by advocating beauty as the primary
objective for himself as an artist. While a scholar at Magdalen
College, Oxford, Wilde was taken by the charm and tranquillity
of his surroundings and saw the college as the ideal setting in
which to create his new persona. He claimed to have 'reformed
fashion and [made] modern dress aesthetically beautiful.' At
the same time, he lost his Irish accent and began to familiarise
himself with the aesthetic theories of his Oxford tutors, Walter
Pater and John Ruskin, as well as the writings of Matthew
Arnold and the philosophy of Hegel.

Wilde left Oxford in 1878 with a first class honours degree and
moved to London, where he rapidly became the centre of an
elite group of artists, writers and performers. This group which
included James McNeill Whistler, William Morris, Lillie
Langtry, George Meredith and Thomas Hardy, as well as

patrons of the arts such as Lord Lytton, Lady Shrewsbury and Lady Dorothy Nevill informally became known as the 'Cult of the Aesthetic'.

In 1882 Wilde lectured on his theories of aestheticism in the United States. He married Constance Lloyd, the daughter of a QC, in 1884 and fathered two sons, Cyril and Vyvyan. The marriage appears to have been one of convenience: Wilde was suffering some financial hardship, and Constance had an income of several hundred pounds per year. This gave him the freedom to go out and about in society, initially accompanied by Constance but more frequently on his own. Over the next three years, he was a familiar figure in London society, famous for his gift of conversational rhetoric.

During this period he had his first homosexual affair, with Robert Ross. This was followed by a succession of short term affairs and encounters with male prostitutes, until 1891 when he met Lord Alfred Douglas, fifteen years his junior and destined to be his one true love. Douglas (or 'Bosie') was, at twenty-one, an aesthete's delight. Wilde's friend, the journalist Frank Harris, described him as 'girlishly pretty, with the beauty of youth, colouring and fair skin.'

The publication of *The Happy Prince and Other Stories* (1888) and *The Picture of Dorian Gray* (1891) established Wilde's reputation as a writer. Wilde's fame was enhanced with the production of his dramatic work – *Lady Windermere's Fan* (February 1892); *A Woman of No Importance* (April 1893); *An Ideal Husband* (January 1895) and *The Importance of Being Earnest* (February 1895). *Salome*, written in French in 1892, was banned by the Lord Chamberlain on the grounds that it featured biblical characters, and was not produced until February 1896 in Paris.

Wilde's affair with Bosie was encountering some difficulties – Douglas, accustomed to a luxurious lifestyle, was a continuing drain on Wilde's financial resources. At the same time, Douglas' father, the Marquis of Queensberry, began a crusade to end the relationship between his son and Wilde. He exchanged letters of insult with his son and with Wilde, confronted them in public and, on the opening night of *The Importance of Being Earnest*, arrived at the theatre carrying a large bouquet of carrots and turnips. He was refused admittance to the performance, but several nights later, left a message for Wilde at the Albemarle Club, accusing him of being a sodomite. Wilde brought a case of libel against Queensberry, which went to court in April 1895. Wilde lost his case, and Queensberry filed a counter-suit, accusing Wilde of 'gross indecency'. Queensberry had gathered evidence in the form of Wilde's letters to Bosie, his published writing (*The Picture of Dorian Gray*, *The Portrait of Mr W.H.*) and various young men who were willing to testify against Wilde. After a second trial (the jury was unable to reach a verdict in the first), Wilde was found guilty and sentenced to two years imprisonment.

Incarcerated in Reading Gaol, Wilde existed in conditions that were the antithesis of everything he believed about beauty and life, with the food inedible, hygiene almost non-existent, proper sleep impossible, and the silence overwhelming. When he was finally allowed the privilege of books and writing material, he produced *De Profundis*, a work that includes a defence of his life, as well as a harsh indictment of Lord Alfred Douglas.

Wilde was released from prison in May 1897, destitute, and moved to France where his only writing of note was *The Ballad of Reading Gaol* (1898), a poem he claimed to have started while in prison. Although the work was widely applauded – numerous editions and translations appeared in England and America and throughout Europe within a matter of weeks – Wilde seemed to have given up his will to live. His doctor forbade him from drinking absinthe – a drink about which Wilde once commented, 'I never could quite accustom myself to absinthe, but it suits my style so well' – but he took no notice. In the last months of his life he suffered from illnesses related to syphilis, and he developed an abscess in his ear, which worsened into meningitis. Oscar Wilde died 30 November 1900, age 46.

What Happens in the Play

Act One. Sir Robert and Lady Gertrude Chiltern are hosting a *soirée* at their home in Grosvenor Square, London. Amongst the arrivals are Lady Markby and her friend, Mrs. Cheveley, who receives a distinctly frosty reception from Lady Chiltern. We discover that the two women knew each other in school. Mrs. Cheveley is particularly looking forward to meeting Sir Robert, a minister in the Foreign Office. When Mrs. Cheveley mentions a 'Baron Arnheim', however, the name causes Sir Robert to jump. Just then, Lord Goring enters and it becomes apparent that he and Mrs. Cheveley know each other. The flirtation between Lord Goring and Miss Mabel Chiltern, Sir Robert's sister is highlighted by Mabel's obvious jealousy of the attention generated by the presence of Mrs. Cheveley.

Managing to speak with Sir Robert alone, Mrs. Cheveley expresses her interest in speculation about the Argentine Canal Company, a scheme that Sir Robert dismisses as 'a common Stock Exchange swindle'. He informs Mrs. Cheveley that he plans to give a negative report on the scheme to the House the following evening. When Sir Robert refuses to withdraw his report, she tells him that she has a letter he wrote to Baron Arnheim. In the letter, written years before when Sir Robert was in a minor government position, he advised the Baron to buy shares in the upcoming Suez Canal, three days prior to the Government announcing its own purchase. In return, the Baron paid Sir Robert £110,000. Mrs. Cheveley leaves, announcing her intention to be in the Ladies Gallery at 11.30 the following night to listen to Sir Robert's speech, promising to reveal the whole scandal if he refuses to withdraw his report.

As the other guests are leaving, Mabel discovers what she thinks is a diamond brooch on the sofa. She shows it to Lord Goring who recognises the jewellery as a bracelet he had given to someone years before, and pockets the piece, asking Mabel to let him know if anyone claims it.

Sir Robert and Lady Chiltern, left alone, discuss the possibility of Sir Robert's withdrawing his report and lending his support

to the Argentine speculation. Lady Chiltern is adamant that Sir
Robert should write to Mrs. Cheveley immediately, rejecting
her demands. He does so, ensuring himself of Lady Chiltern's
continuing love and respect.

Act Two. The following morning, Lord Goring and Sir Robert,
who is in a high state of agitation, are discussing the scandal
that will ensue, if Sir Robert does not give in to Mrs. Cheveley.
Lord Goring is surprised that Lady Chiltern does not know of
the situation, but Sir Robert is determined to keep the
information about the Suez speculation from her, worried that
she will renounce him if she knew of his past actions. Lady
Chiltern enters, just as Sir Robert is leaving. She takes the
opportunity to discuss Mrs. Cheveley's request with Lord
Goring, and repeats her views on morality and ethics. Lady
Markby and Mrs. Cheveley arrive on the pretext of finding
Mrs. Cheveley's brooch. Lady Markby leaves to call on another
friend, giving Mrs. Cheveley the chance to reveal Sir Robert's
fraudulent actions, and to repeat her threat to publicly expose
him. Sir Robert enters in time to hear the end of this warning,
and is forced to admit everything to his wife. As he expects,
she rejects him, telling him that she had always regarded him
as her ideal. This compels him to defend himself, stating that
although women place men on pedestals, they are only human,
deserving compassion and understanding instead of
recriminations.

Act Three. Lord Goring, arriving home, discovers a letter from
Lady Chiltern, asking to see him, but written in rather
ambiguous language. Lord Caversham, his father, arrives and
immediately begins taxing his son about his unmarried state,
clearly a well-worn argument between the two. Lord Goring
manoeuvres his father into the smoking room in order to clear
the way for Lady Chiltern. The footman mistakenly admits
Mrs. Cheveley who finds the letter from Lady Chiltern. She is
about to steal it when the butler interrupts her to show her
into the drawing room. Lord Goring is showing Lord
Caversham out when Sir Robert arrives. Thinking that Lady
Chiltern is waiting for him in the drawing room, Lord Goring

is desperate to send Sir Robert away; however, Sir Robert is just as desperate to seek Lord Goring's commiseration for his situation. As Sir Robert is about to reveal his plans for the debate on the Argentine Canal that evening, Mrs. Cheveley, who has been listening from the drawing room, knocks a chair over. Outraged to discover that Lord Goring has been entertaining the woman who is threatening to ruin his career, Sir Robert leaves the house. Mrs. Cheveley mentions the brooch that she lost the previous evening, and Lord Goring tells her that he found it. He shows it to her and places it on her wrist as a bracelet, accusing her of stealing it from his cousin and threatening to call the police unless she returns Sir Robert's letter. She does so, but also manages to steal Lady Chiltern's letter as the butler shows her the door.

Act Four. The following morning, Lord Goring is at Grosvenor Square, waiting to see Sir Robert or Lady Chiltern or Mabel. Instead, the first person he encounters is Lord Caversham, who asks him again about his plans for marriage. Lord Goring promises to be engaged before lunchtime that day, and his father tells him about the article in *The Times*, complimenting Sir Robert's denouncement of the Argentine Canal scheme. Mabel enters and carries on a lively conversation with Lord Caversham, quite pointedly ignoring Lord Goring's attempts to speak with her. She is clearly put out by the fact that he missed his appointment with her that morning, and that he has not yet proposed marriage. He does so, and agrees to meet her in the conservatory after he has spoken with Lady Chiltern. He tells Lady Chiltern that Mrs. Cheveley did return Sir Robert's letter the previous evening, and encourages her to tell her husband about the letter she sent to Lord Goring. He is forced to admit that Mrs. Cheveley stole the letter from his home, and that she plans to send the letter to Sir Robert.

Sir Robert enters, having received the letter, but assumes it was meant for him originally. He takes the message to mean that Lady Chiltern is willing to forgive him for his past error. She does so, but she also wants him to retire from public life. Just then, Lord Caversham re-enters, bearing a message from the

Prime Minister, offering Sir Robert a seat in the Cabinet, which he reluctantly declines. Sir Robert leaves to write his letter of resignation from the Government. Lord Goring convinces Lady Chiltern that Sir Robert should be allowed to keep his place as a Government Minister. Sir Robert expresses his gratitude to Lord Goring for his support and friendship; however, when Lord Goring requests Mabel's hand in marriage, Sir Robert refuses on the grounds that Lord Goring was entertaining Mrs. Cheveley in his rooms during the previous evening. Lady Chiltern solves the problem by confessing her own part in those events; that the letter Sir Robert received that morning had actually been written to Lord Goring, and she was the woman he was expecting. Sir Robert gives his consent for the marriage of Mabel to Lord Goring, and he and Lady Chiltern re-affirm their love for each other and the beginning of their new life together.

Wilde and Society Melodrama

An Ideal Husband is the last of three social melodramas Wilde wrote between the publication of *The Picture of Dorian Gray* and the premiere of *The Importance of Being Earnest*. *Lady Windermere's Fan*, *A Woman of No Importance* and *An Ideal Husband* are illustrative of the processes that determined Wilde's dramatic voice.

Social melodrama developed during the latter half of the nineteenth-century, although its roots can be clearly seen in the sentimental drama of the eighteenth-century. These dramas were inspired by the view that human beings are innately virtuous and endowed with a strong moral sense. Society melodrama, as written by Wilde, views these attributes as masks donned by the aristocracy. Wilde's *modus operandi*, then, is to expose those masks as such, and examine the reality that lies underneath. Within the dramatic world of *An Ideal Husband*, the playwright not only questions the consequences of an ethical lapse on a man's personal relationships, but widens the scope of his examination to encompass the very public world of the Government. The characters are written

with Wilde's customary penetrating wit and keen social observations, and are developed to highlight the author's critique of
false ideals and illusions.

What separates *An Ideal Husband* from *Lady Windermere's Fan*
and *A Woman of No Importance* is the intense scrutiny afforded
to both sides of the debate. Unlike *A Woman of No Importance*,
Wilde does not identify any single character for condemnation.
Instead, they are permitted to continue as before, in much the
same way that contemporary ambitious politicians had to
resort to hypocrisy and artifice in order to achieve their goals.

Wilde was very aware of the demands for absolute moral beha-
viour that late-Victorian society placed on its political leaders.
The fictitious Argentine Canal scheme at the crux of *An Ideal
Husband* mirrors a contemporary French scandal over the
Panama Canal. Wilde's friend Frank Harris also claimed that
the idea for *An Ideal Husband* came from a story he once told
to Wilde about Benjamin Disraeli earning quite a lot of money
by entrusting the Rothschilds with the purchase of the Suez
Canal shares. If true, this story, along with the scandal in the
French government, presented Wilde with an ideal opportunity
for an explication of how corruption infiltrates and becomes
omnipresent within the personal and political identity of Sir
Robert Chiltern. Typically of Wilde's dramaturgy, he is not
particularly concerned with the guilt of the protagonist;
instead, he is more interested in revealing the indiscretions of
the political system that harbours guilt such as Sir Robert's.

With unerring accuracy, Wilde identified and encapsulated the
sanctimonious morality of the Victorian world – the world that
was soon going to expose and consume him. The emphasis in
his play on hidden secrets which must not be revealed chimes
well with the realities of homosexual life in Victorian society.

First produced at the Haymarket Theatre on 3 January 1895,
An Ideal Husband was received with enthusiasm by audiences
and with reservation by many of the critics. Clement Scott,
writing in the *Illustrated London News* on 12 January 1895,
noted the current popularity of Wilde, especially in what he

termed the 'author's method and trick of talk.' Although acknowledging the overall impact of the play, he nonetheless felt compelled to censure the cleverness of the language: 'There is scarcely one Oscar Wildeism uttered in the new Haymarket play that will bear one minute's analysis, but for all that they tickle the ears of the groundlings, and are accepted as stage cleverness.' By contrast, Bernard Shaw, wrote in the *Saturday Review* that he was 'the only person in London who cannot sit down and write an Oscar Wilde play at will.' What is clear from these examples is the actuality of Wilde's skill in writing witty dialogue. Frequently criticised for the jocose style of his plays, it was this mode of expression that made his writing unique. Bernard Shaw went on to describe Wilde as 'our only thorough playwright. He plays with everything: with wit, with philosophy, with drama, with actors and audience, with the whole theatre.' There is a good deal of truth in this assessment. Wilde often used standard melodramatic conventions in his writing; however, he was less interested in emotional insight than in a witty turn of phrase. Plays like *An Ideal Husband* may have been formulated on a foundation of moral examination, but it is the clever aphorisms and droll observations on life and society that elevate the play above other contemporary melodramas. For this reason, the play enjoyed a successful run of 111 performances until it was withdrawn the day following Wilde's arrest. It was a tribute to Wilde's deftness with a turn of phrase that audiences appreciated and respected the epigrammatic framing of what was a familiar tale of intrigue and extortion.

Cult of the Aesthete and the New Dandyism

One result of the renewed interest given to beauty and romanticism by the aesthetes in the latter half of the nineteenth-century was a concentration on language, personal dress and bearing, and it was characteristic of this artistic renaissance that its followers celebrated a new found love of the artificial. Nature was no longer regarded as supreme; instead, the improvements on Nature – cosmetics, heightened language, and self-regard – were the attributes that were revered. A new urbanity was embraced by the aesthetes, and Wilde's developing art of speaking endeared him to some of the best houses and circles in London.

Many within Wilde's circle of friends believed it was the time for a renewed concentration on art and beauty. During the 1880's and 1890's, the literary and theatrical worlds had focused on the unrelenting urban naturalism of Zola and his followers, a form which paid strict attention to scientific observation. A movement towards art for its own sake allowed a creative divergence from what was the current trend of writing. Artists and poets began to take a pastoral view towards the artifice that existed in the towns and cities, and found a new romance and life in the inanimate trappings of the elite. By celebrating the facade created by his friends and admirers, Wilde illustrated the artificiality of their lives.

Prior to his marriage to Constance Lloyd in 1884, Wilde had continual difficulty financing his love of opulence and indulgence. He had a fondness for fine art and first editions; he was extremely vain, and made his personal fashion central to his concerns – to the point of overdressing. Craving pleasure, he sought it from every aspect of his life; unfortunately, he was constantly in debt and forced to borrow in order to maintain his extravagant lifestyle. Having married Constance, her annual income allowed him to pursue this life of lavishness and to perfect his art of being Oscar Wilde.

This self-awareness of the external persona found its way into Wilde's dramatic writing in the shape of the 'dandy'. Like Wilde himself, these characters (Lord Goring in *An Ideal Husband*, Algernon Moncrieff in *The Importance of Being Earnest*) perfected the art of posing, a principle which expressed itself not only in clothing but also in the attitude, intellect and temperament of the individual. This is clearly illustrated by Wilde's description of Lord Goring, a young man of

> thirty-four, but always says he is younger. A well-bred, expressionless face. He is clever, but would not like to be

thought so. A flawless dandy, he would be annoyed if he were considered romantic. He plays with life, and is on perfectly good terms with the world. He is fond of being misunderstood. It gives him a post of vantage.

Lord Goring is the quintessence of a late nineteenth-century dandy – he is the despair of his father, Lord Caversham, who describes him as 'heartless', 'conceited' and 'good-for-nothing'. Lord Caversham wants his son to marry, as he perceives Lord Goring to be wasting his life ('bachelors are not fashionable anymore'), and does not understand the attraction of London Society:

> Lord Caversham. The thing has gone to the dogs, a lot of damned nobodies talking about nothing.
> Lord Goring. I love talking about nothing, father. It is the only thing I know anything about.
> Lord Caversham. You seem to me to be living entirely for pleasure.
> Lord Goring. What else is there to live for, father? Nothing ages like happiness.

Lord Goring revels in the minutiae of style; Wilde indicates that 'his are all the delicate fopperies of Fashion. One sees that he stands in immediate relation to modern life, makes it indeed, and so masters it. He is the first well-dressed philosopher in the history of thought.' Goring reminds his butler, Phipps, to have a word with his florist, as she is preparing buttonholes that are not trivial enough for a Thursday. He is candid about his faults:

> Mabel. You are always telling me your bad qualities, Lord Goring.
> Lord Goring. I have only told you half of them as yet, Miss Mabel!
> Mabel. Are the others very bad?
> Lord Goring. Quite dreadful! When I think of them at night I go to sleep at once.
> Mabel. Well, I delight in your bad qualities. I wouldn't have you part with one of them.

This perversity of exchange is indicative of the relativity in the rules of the dandy, what both Sir Robert and Mrs Cheveley call 'the game of life'. In this world it is preferable to avoid absolutes, the circumstance of the Chilterns being a case in point. Of all the characters in *An Ideal Husband*, only Mabel Chiltern and Lord Goring do not mention what a man or a woman should or should not be. As non-conforming individuals, they are released from the necessity of compliance with the established norms. In doing so, they embrace the values of 'Dandyism'.

Concurrent with his own self-presentation, Lord Goring proves to be a keen observer of human nature – certainly of those who populate his dramatic world. In *Phrases and Philosophies for the Use of the Young*, Wilde stated 'to expect the unexpected shows a thoroughly modern intellect,' and this seems to be the philosophy with which he endowed Lord Goring. He is the catalyst who resolves the various conflicts that arise in the play – Mrs Cheveley's blackmail plans, Sir Robert's ethical dilemmas, and Lady Chiltern's unwavering morality. He delivers one serious 'philosopher's' speech, in which he shows a full understanding of the situation and the personalities of the characters involved:

> A man's life is of more value than a woman's. It has larger issues, wider scope, greater ambitions. A woman's life revolves in curves of emotions. It is upon lines of intellect that a man's life progresses.

Although it has proved problematic for critics, in this speech Goring actually demonstrates an astute perception of the Chiltern's marriage and their personal responses. Although seemingly contradictory to the play's argument against the division of male and female spheres, it is important to bear in mind the central principles of dandyism – that all rules are variable and subject to change. Lord Goring adapts his approach based on the circumstances he encounters. All truths are relative, and the successful dandy disengages himself from what appears to be the unequivocal truth. As Goring tells Phipps in Act III, 'falsehoods [are] the truths of other people.'

The Art of the Play

Wilde's aesthetic philosophy is as much in evidence in *An Ideal Husband* as in any of his other plays. He wrote in *The Critic as Artist* that 'all over England there is a Renaissance of the decorative Arts. Ugliness has had its day. Even in the houses of the rich there is taste.' This idea is illustrated in Wilde's embellished stage directions, which describe the characters in terms of works of art. While this may give some insight into his dramaturgy, the descriptions are probably more correctly seen as a dramatic expression of Wilde's statement on art: 'For there are not many arts, but one art merely.' As an example, he describes Mrs Cheveley as 'a work of art. . .but showing the influence of too many schools', a description that underlines the inconsistency of her character.

Where Wilde is truly impressive, of course, is in his command of the language. His characters are exceedingly witty, and there is a sense of craftsmanship throughout the work. Even the critics who were most damning of the play generally agreed on the quality of the language, although not always positively. A.B. Walkley writing in *The Speaker* on 12 January 1895 described the play as 'a strepitous, polychromatic, scintillant affair, dextrous as a conjurer's trick of legerdemain, clever with a cleverness so excessive as to be almost monstrous and uncanny'. The audience who were attending the performances at the Haymarket, however, were enthusiastic with their response to the complexity of the writing. In addition to their unquestioned appreciation of his skill, audiences also enjoyed Wilde's challenge to the traditional ideals of marriage and relationships between men and women.

Wilde's literary art can be fully realised when his writing is seen in relation to not only the social and dramatic milieu of the late nineteenth-century, but also when presented to audiences a full century later. Oliver Parker's film of *An Ideal Husband* (1999) resonates with contemporary spectators by allowing them to view the issues at the heart of the story. An American critic began his review of the film as: 'Shameful pasts. Secret affairs. Astonishing revelations. Political intrigue.' One could be forgiven for thinking that this could have been a review of current government personalities and events, on both sides of the Atlantic. What the film is able to provide is a juncture between Wilde's often world-weary view of London society and the cynicism of audiences at the end of the millennium.

For Further Reading

There are a wide range of texts that examine the life, work, family and art of Oscar Wilde. Many older works, such as Frank Harris' *Oscar Wilde* (original publication 1916, republished by Carroll and Graf, 1992) take the form of biographical reminiscences and are frequently biased by personal friendship. Richard Ellman's *Oscar Wilde* (Hamish Hamilton, 1987) presents a detailed account of Wilde's life and is far more useful as a reference. Kerry Powell's book *Oscar Wilde and the Theatre of the 1890's* (Cambridge University Press, 1990) presents a modern perspective on the plays and their place in the Victorian theatre. Michael Patrick Gillespie examines specific issues pertaining to the plays in *Oscar Wilde and the Poetics of Ambiguity* (University Press of Florida, 1997); his chapter on 'Reviewing the Dandy in *The Importance of Being Earnest*' is particularly notable. *The Cambridge Companion to Oscar* Wilde (edited by Peter Raby, Cambridge University Press, 1997) provides a range of essays by contemporary critics and academics. Sos Eltis' *Revising Wilde: Society and Subversion in the Plays of Oscar Wilde* (Clarendon Press, 1996) contains detailed discussions of the dramatic works, including an overview of the early versions of *An Ideal Husband*. Rodney Shewan's *Oscar Wilde: Art and Egotism* (Macmillan, 1977) and Michael Hardwick's *The Drake Guide to Oscar Wilde* (Drake Publishers, 1973) both provide interesting analysis of the plays. Karl Beckson's (ed.) *Oscar Wilde: The Critical Heritage* (Routledge and Kegan Paul, 1970) offers a selection of original dramatic reviews.

It is difficult to discuss *An Ideal Husband* without considering Wilde's involvement with the 'Art for Art's Sake' cult. Julia Prewitt Brown's *Cosmopolitan Criticism: Oscar Wilde's Philosophy of*

Art (University Press of Virginia, 1997) considers Wilde's development of his theories of art and examines how these ideas are manifested in his literature. Carl Woodring's *Nature into Art: Cultural Transformations in Nineteenth-Century Britain* (Harvard University Press, 1989) provides a clear history and analysis of the aesthetic movement. He not only reflects on Wilde, but other artists with whom Wilde was associated, e.g. Whistler, Symons, and Pater. Volume 4 of Arnold Hauser's *The Social History of Art* (Routledge, 1999) further places the aesthetic trend into its social context. For an interesting exploration of nineteenth-century artistic motivation, Barnaby Conrad's *Absinthe: History in a Bottle* (Chronicle Books, 1988) gives a fascinating account of those artists and poets (including Jarry, Verlaine, Van Gogh and Degas, as well as Wilde) who helped to make the drink a symbol for decadence.

Wilde: Key Dates

1854	Wilde is born on 16 October in Dublin. Older brother William born in 1852; younger sister Isola born in 1857
1864-71	Boarding student at Portora Royal School in Enniskillen
1867	Death of sister, Isola Wilde
1871-74	Student at Trinity College, Dublin
1874-78	Scholarship student at Magdalen College, Oxford
1876	Death of Sir William Wilde (father) on 19 April
1877	Tour of Greece with Trinity Professor Mahaffy
1878	Moves to London and begins working as a journalist for the society paper, *The World*
1880	Publication of his first play, *Vera, or the Nihilists*
1881	Publication of his first collection of poems
1882	Lecture tour of the United States
1884	Marries Constance Lloyd on 29 May
1885	Birth of son, Cyril
1886	Birth of son, Vyvyan. Wilde's first homosexual affair, with Robert Ross
1887-89	Editor of *The Woman's World*
1888	Publication of *The Happy Prince and Other Tales*
1890	First publication of *The Picture of Dorian Gray* in *Lippincott's Magazine*

1891	Publication of *Intentions*, which included 'The Decay of Lying', first published in *The Nineteenth Century*; 'Pen, Pencil and Poison' in *Fortnightly Review*; 'The Portrait of Mr W.H.' in *Blackwood's Magazine*. Publication of *The Picture of Dorian Gray* in book form. Publication of *A House of Pomegranates*. Meets Lord Alfred Douglas (Bosie). Writes *Salome* in Paris
1892	*Lady Windermere's Fan* produced at St James's Theatre, 22 February. Writes *A Woman of No Importance*
1893	*A Woman of No Importance* produced at the Haymarket Theatre, 19 April. *Lady Windermere's Fan* published.
1894	*Salome* published in French. *A Woman of No Importance* published. Writes *An Ideal Husband*, *The Importance of Being Earnest*, *A Florentine Tragedy*
1895	*An Ideal Husband* produced at the Haymarket Theatre, 3 January. *The Importance of Being Earnest* produced at St James's Theatre, 14 February. Brings libel suit again Marquis of Queensbury for insulting note. Wilde loses his case and is brought to trial for 'gross indecency'. He is found guilty and sentenced to two years hard labour
1896	Lady Jane Wilde (mother) dies, 3 February. *Salome* produced at Theatre de l'Oeuvre, Paris, 11 February
1897	Writes *De Profundis* while in prison. Released from prison, 9 May
1898	*The Ballad of Reading Gaol* published, January, under the pseudonym C.3.3.
1899	*An Ideal Husband* and *The Importance of Being Earnest* published
1900	Wilde dies in Paris on 30 November of meningitis, probably caused by tertiary syphillis

AN IDEAL HUSBAND

To
FRANK HARRIS
a slight tribute
to his power and distinction as an artist
his chivalry and nobility as a friend

The Persons of the Play

THE EARL OF CAVERSHAM, K.G.
VISCOUNT GORING, *his son*
SIR ROBERT CHILTERN, *Bart, Under-Secretary for Foreign
    Affairs*
VICOMTE DE NANJAC, *Attaché at the French Embassy in London*
MR MONTFORD
MASON, *Butler to Sir Robert Chiltern*
PHIPPS, *Lord Goring's servant*
JAMES, *Footman*
HAROLD, *Footman*
LADY CHILTERN
LADY MARKBY
THE COUNTESS OF BASILDON
MRS MARCHMONT
MISS MABEL CHILTERN, *Sir Robert Chiltern's sister*
MRS CHEVELEY

The Scenes of the Play

*Act I: the Octagon Room in Sir Robert Chiltern's house in
Grosvenor Square*

Act II: Morning-Room in Sir Robert Chiltern's house

Act III: the Library of Lord Goring's house in Curzon Street

Act IV: same as Act II

Time: the present

Place: London

The action of the play is completed within twenty-four hours

FIRST ACT

Scene: the Octagon Room at Sir Robert Chiltern's house in Grosvenor Square.

The room is brilliantly lighted and full of guests. At the top of the staircase stands LADY CHILTERN, *a woman of grave Greek beauty, about twenty-seven years of age. She receives the guests as they come up. Over the well of the staircase hangs a great chandelier with wax lights, which illumine a large eighteenth-century French tapestry – representing the Triumph of Love, from a design by Boucher – that is stretched on the staircase wall. On the right is the entrance to the music-room. The sound of a string quartette is faintly heard. The entrance on the left leads to other reception-rooms.* MRS MARCHMONT *and* LADY BASILDON, *two very pretty women, are seated together on a Louis Seize sofa. They are types of exquisite fragility. Their affectation of manner has a delicate charm. Watteau would have loved to paint them.*

MRS MARCHMONT. Going on to the Hartlocks' tonight, Margaret?

LADY BASILDON. I suppose so. Are you?

MRS MARCHMONT. Yes. Horribly tedious parties they give, don't they?

LADY BASILDON. Horribly tedious! Never know why I go. Never know why I go anywhere.

MRS MARCHMONT. I come here to be educated.

LADY BASILDON. Ah! I hate being educated!

MRS MARCHMONT. So do I. It puts one almost on a level with the commercial classes, doesn't it? But dear Gertrude Chiltern is always telling me that I should have some serious purpose in life. So I come here to try to find one.

LADY BASILDON (*looking round through her lorgnette*). I don't see anybody here tonight whom one could possibly call a serious purpose. The man who took me in to dinner talked to me about his wife the whole time.

MRS MARCHMONT. How very trivial of him!

LADY BASILDON. Terribly trivial! What did your man talk about?

MRS MARCHMONT. About myself.

LADY BASILDON (*languidly*). And were you interested?

MRS MARCHMONT (*shaking her head*). Not in the smallest degree.

LADY BASILDON. What martyrs we are, dear Margaret!

MRS MARCHMONT (*rising*). And how well it becomes us, Olivia!

They rise and go towards the music-room. The VICOMTE DE NANJAC, *a young attaché known for his neckties and his Anglomania, approaches with a low bow, and enters into conversation.*

MASON (*announcing guests from the top of the staircase*). Mr and Lady Jane Barford. Lord Caversham.

Enter LORD CAVERSHAM, *an old gentleman of seventy, wearing the riband and star of the Garter. A fine Whig type. Rather like a portrait by Lawrence.*

LORD CAVERSHAM. Good evening, Lady Chiltern! Has my good-for-nothing young son been here?

LADY CHILTERN (*smiling*). I don't think Lord Goring has arrived yet.

MABEL CHILTERN (*coming up to* LORD CAVERSHAM). Why do you call Lord Goring good-for-nothing?

MABEL CHILTERN *is a perfect example of the English type of prettiness, the apple-blossom type. She has all the fragrance and freedom of a flower. There is ripple after ripple of sunlight in her hair, and the little mouth, with its parted lips, is expectant, like the mouth of a child. She has the fascinating tyranny of youth, and the astonishing courage of innocence. To sane people she is not reminiscent of any work of art. But she is really like a Tanagra statuette, and would be rather annoyed if she were told so.*

LORD CAVERSHAM. Because he leads such an idle life.

MABEL CHILTERN. How can you say such a thing? Why, he rides in the Row at ten o'clock in the morning, goes to the Opera three times a week, changes his clothes at least five times a day, and dines out every night of the season. You don't call that leading an idle life, do you?

LORD CAVERSHAM (*looking at her with a kindly twinkle in his eye*). You are a very charming young lady!

MABEL CHILTERN. How sweet of you to say that, Lord Caversham! Do come to us more often. You know we are always at home on Wednesdays, and you look so well with your star!

LORD CAVERSHAM. Never go anywhere now. Sick of London Society. Shouldn't mind being introduced to my own tailor; he always votes on the right side. But object strongly to being sent down to dinner with my wife's milliner. Never could stand Lady Caversham's bonnets.

MABEL CHILTERN. Oh, I love London Society! I think it has immensely improved. It is entirely composed now of beautiful idiots and brilliant lunatics. Just what Society should be.

LORD CAVERSHAM. Hum! Which is Goring? Beautiful idiot, or the other thing?

MABEL CHILTERN (*gravely*). I have been obliged for the present to put Lord Goring into a class quite by himself. But he is developing charmingly!

LORD CAVERSHAM. Into what?

MABEL CHILTERN (*with a little curtsey*). I hope to let you know very soon, Lord Caversham!

MASON (*announcing guests*). Lady Markby. Mrs Cheveley.

Enter LADY MARKBY *and* MRS CHEVELEY. LADY MARKBY *is a pleasant, kindly, popular woman, with grey hair à la marquise and good lace.* MRS CHEVELEY, *who accompanies her, is tall and rather slight. Lips very thin and highly-coloured, a line of scarlet on a pallid face. Venetian red hair, aquiline nose, and long throat. Rouge accentuates the natural paleness of her complexion. Grey-green eyes that move restlessly. She is in heliotrope, with diamonds. She looks rather like an orchid, and makes great demands on one's curiosity. In all her movements she is extremely graceful. A work of art, on the whole, but showing the influence of too many schools.*

LADY MARKBY. Good evening, dear Gertrude! So kind of you to let me bring my friend, Mrs Cheveley. Two such charming women should know each other!

LADY CHILTERN (*advances toward* MRS CHEVELEY *with a sweet smile. Then suddenly stops, and bows rather distantly*). I think Mrs Cheveley and I have met before. I did not know she had married a second time.

LADY MARKBY (*genially*). Ah, nowadays people marry as often as they can, don't they? It is most fashionable. (*To* DUCHESS OF MARYBOROUGH.) Dear Duchess, and how is the Duke? Brain still weak, I suppose? Well, that is only to be expected, is it not? His good father was just the same. There is nothing like race, is there?

MRS CHEVELEY (*playing with her fan*). But have we really met before, Lady Chiltern? I can't remember where. I have been out of England for so long.

LADY CHILTERN. We were at school together, Mrs Cheveley.

MRS CHEVELEY (*superciliously*). Indeed? I have forgotten all about my schooldays. I have a vague impression that they were detestable.

LADY CHILTERN (*coldly*). I am not surprised!

MRS CHEVELEY (*in her sweetest manner*). Do you know, I am quite looking forward to meeting your clever husband, Lady Chiltern. Since he has been at the Foreign Office, he has been so much talked of in Vienna. They actually succeed in spelling his name right in the newspapers. That in itself is fame, on the continent.

LADY CHILTERN. I hardly think there will be much in common between you and my husband, Mrs Cheveley!

Moves away.

VICOMTE DE NANJAC. Ah! chère Madame, quelle surprise! I have not seen you since Berlin!

MRS CHEVELEY. Not since Berlin, Vicomte. Five years ago!

VICOMTE DE NANJAC. And you are younger and more beautiful than ever. How do you manage it?

MRS CHEVELEY. By making it a rule only to talk to perfectly charming people like yourself

VICOMTE DE NANJAC. Ah! you flatter me. You butter me, as they say here.

MRS CHEVELEY. Do they say that here? How dreadful of them!

VICOMTE DE NANJAC. Yes, they have a wonderful language. It should he more widely known.

SIR ROBERT CHILTERN *enters. A man of forty, but looking somewhat younger. Clean-shaven, with finely-cut features, dark-haired and dark-eyed. A personality of mark. Not popular – few personalities are. But intensely admired by the few, and deeply respected by the many. The note of his manner is that of perfect distinction, with a slight touch of pride. One feels that he is conscious of the success he has made in life. A nervous temperament, with a tired look. The firmly-chiselled mouth and chin contrast strikingly with the romantic expression in the deep-set eyes. The variance is suggestive of an almost complete separation of passion and intellect, as though thought and emotion were each isolated in its own sphere through some violence of will-power. There is nervousness in the nostrils, and in the pale, thin, pointed hands. It would be inaccurate to call him picturesque. Picturesqueness cannot survive the House of Commons. But Vandyck would have liked to have painted his head.*

SIR ROBERT CHILTERN. Good evening, Lady Markby!
I hope you have brought Sir John with you?

LADY MARKBY. Oh! I have brought a much more charming person than Sir John. Sir John's temper since he has taken seriously to politics has become quite unbearable. Really, now that the House of Commons is trying to become useful, it does a great deal of harm.

SIR ROBERT CHILTERN. I hope not, Lady Markby. At any rate we do our best to waste the public time, don't we? But who is this charming person you have been kind enough to bring to us?

LADY MARKBY. Her name is Mrs Cheveley. One of the
Dorsetshire Cheveleys, I suppose. But I really don't know.
Families are so mixed nowadays. Indeed, as a rule, every-
body turns out to be somebody else.

SIR ROBERT CHILTERN. Mrs Cheveley? I seem to know the
name.

LADY MARKBY. She has just arrived from Vienna.

SIR ROBERT CHILTERN. Ah! yes. I think I know whom you
mean.

LADY MARKBY. Oh! she goes everywhere there, and has such
pleasant scandals about all her friends. I really must go to
Vienna next winter. I hope there is a good chef at the
Embassy.

SIR ROBERT CHILTERN. If there is not, the Ambassador will
certainly have to be recalled. Pray point out Mrs Cheveley
to me. I should like to see her.

LADY MARKBY. Let me introduce you. (*To* MRS CHEVELEY.)
My dear, Sir Robert Chiltern is dying to know you!

SIR ROBERT CHILTERN (*bowing*). Every one is dying to
know the brilliant Mrs Cheveley. Our attachés at Vienna
write to us about nothing else.

MRS CHEVELEY. Thank you, Sir Robert. An acquaintance
that begins with a compliment is sure to develop into a real
friendship. It starts in the right manner. And I find that I
know Lady Chiltern already.

SIR ROBERT CHILTERN. Really?

MRS CHEVELEY. Yes. She has just reminded me that we were
at school together. I remember it perfectly now. She always
got the good conduct prize. I have a distinct recollection of
Lady Chiltern always getting the good conduct prize!

SIR ROBERT CHILTERN (*smiling*). And what prizes did you
get, Mrs Cheveley?

MRS CHEVELEY. My prizes came a little later on in life.
I don't think any of them were for good conduct. I forget!

SIR ROBERT CHILTERN. I am sure they were for something
charming!

MRS CHEVELEY. I don't know that women are always rewarded for being charming. I think they are usually punished for it! Certainly, more women grow old nowadays through the faithfulness of their admirers than through anything else! At least that is the only way I can account for the terribly haggard look of most of your pretty women in London!

SIR ROBERT CHILTERN. What an appalling philosophy that sounds! To attempt to classify you, Mrs Cheveley, would be an impertinence. But may I ask, at heart, are you an optimist or a pessimist? Those seem to be the only two fashionable religions left to us nowadays.

MRS CHEVELEY. Oh, I'm neither. Optimism begins in a broad grin, and Pessimism ends with blue spectacles. Besides, they are both of them merely poses.

SIR ROBERT CHILTERN. You prefer to be natural?

MRS CHEVELEY. Sometimes. But it is such a very difficult pose to keep up.

SIR ROBERT CHILTERN. What would those modern psycho-logical novelists, of whom we hear so much, say to such a theory as that?

MRS CHEVELEY. Ah! the strength of women comes from the fact that psychology cannot explain us. Men can be analysed, women . . . merely adored.

SIR ROBERT CHILTERN. You think science cannot grapple with the problem of women?

MRS CHEVELEY. Science can never grapple with the irrational. That is why it has no future before it, in this world.

SIR ROBERT CHILTERN. And women represent the irrational.

MRS CHEVELEY. Well-dressed women do.

SIR ROBERT CHILTERN (*with a polite bow*). I fear I could hardly agree with you there. But do sit down. And now tell me, what makes you leave your brilliant Vienna for our gloomy London – or perhaps the question is indiscreet?

MRS CHEVELEY. Questions are never indiscreet. Answers sometimes are.

SIR ROBERT CHILTERN. Well, at any rate, may I know if it is politics or pleasure ?

MRS CHEVELEY. Politics are my only pleasure. You see nowadays it is not fashionable to flirt till one is forty, or to be romantic till one is forty-five, so we poor women who are under thirty, or say we are, have nothing open to us but politics or philanthropy. And philanthropy seems to me to have become simply the refuge of people who wish to annoy their fellow-creatures. I prefer politics. I think they are more . . . becoming!

SIR ROBERT CHILTERN. A political life is a noble career!

MRS CHEVELEY. Sometimes. And sometimes it is a clever game, Sir Robert. And sometimes it is a great nuisance.

SIR ROBERT CHILTERN. Which do you find it?

MRS CHEVELEY. I? A combination of all three.

Drops her fan.

SIR ROBERT CHILTERN (*picks up fan*). Allow me!

MRS CHEVELEY. Thanks.

SIR ROBERT CHILTERN. But you have not told me yet what makes you honour London so suddenly. Our season is almost over.

MRS CHEVELEY. Oh! I don't care about the London season! It is too matrimonial. People are either hunting for husbands, or hiding from them. I wanted to meet you. It is quite true. You know what a woman's curiosity is. Almost as great as a man's! I wanted immensely to meet you, and . . . to ask you to do something for me.

SIR ROBERT CHILTERN. I hope it is not a little thing, Mrs Cheveley. I find that little things are so very difficult to do.

MRS CHEVELEY (*after a moment's reflection*). No, I don't think it is quite a little thing.

SIR ROBERT CHILTERN. I am so glad. Do tell me what it is.

MRS CHEVELEY. Later on. (*Rises.*) And now may I walk through your beautiful house? I hear your pictures are charming. Poor Baron Arnheim – you remember the Baron? – used to tell me you had some wonderful Corots.

SIR ROBERT CHILTERN (*with an almost imperceptible start*). Did you know Baron Arnheim well?

MRS CHEVELEY (*smiling*). Intimately. Did you?

SIR ROBERT CHILTERN. At one time.

MRS CHEVELEY. Wonderful man, wasn't he?

SIR ROBERT CHILTERN (*after a pause*). He was very remarkable, in many ways.

MRS CHEVELEY. I often think it such a pity he never wrote his memoirs. They would have been most interesting.

SIR ROBERT CHILTERN. Yes: he knew men and cities well, like the old Greek.

MRS CHEVELEY. Without the dreadful disadvantage of having a Penelope waiting at home for him.

MASON. Lord Goring.

Enter LORD GORING. *Thirty-four, but always says he is younger. A well-bred, expressionless face. He is clever, but would not like to be thought so. A flawless dandy, he would be annoyed if he were considered romantic. He plays with life, and is on perfectly good terms with the world. He is fond of being misunderstood. It gives him a post of vantage.*

SIR ROBERT CHILTERN. Good evening, my dear Arthur! Mrs Cheveley, allow me to introduce to you Lord Goring, the idlest man in London.

MRS CHEVELEY. I have met Lord Goring before.

LORD GORING (*bowing*). I did not think you would remember me, Mrs Cheveley.

MRS CHEVELEY. My memory is under admirable control. And are you still a bachelor?

LORD GORING. I . . . believe so.

MRS CHEVELEY. How very romantic!

LORD GORING. Oh! I am not at all romantic. I am not old enough. I leave romance to my seniors.

SIR ROBERT CHILTERN. Lord Goring is the result of Boodle's Club, Mrs Cheveley.

MRS CHEVELEY. He reflects every credit on the institution.

LORD GORING. May I ask are you staying in London long?

MRS CHEVELEY. That depends partly on the weather, partly on the cooking, and partly on Sir Robert.

SIR ROBERT CHILTERN. You are not going to plunge us into a European war, I hope?

MRS CHEVELEY. There is no danger, at present!

She nods to LORD GORING, *with a look of amusement in her eyes, and goes out with* SIR ROBERT CHILTERN. LORD GORING *saunters over to* MABEL CHILTERN.

MABEL CHILTERN. You are very late!

LORD GORING. Have you missed me?

MABEL CHILTERN. Awfully!

LORD GORING. Then I am sorry I did not stay away longer. I like being missed.

MABEL CHILTERN. How very selfish of you!

LORD GORING. I am very selfish.

MABEL CHILTERN. You are always telling me of your bad qualities, Lord Goring.

LORD GORING. I have only told you half of them as yet, Miss Mabel!

MABEL CHILTERN. Are the others very bad?

LORD GORING. Quite dreadful! When I think of them at night I go to sleep at once.

MABEL CHILTERN. Well, I delight in your bad qualities. I wouldn't have you part with one of them.

LORD GORING. How very nice of you! But then you are always nice. By the way, I want to ask you a question, Miss

Mabel. Who brought Mrs Cheveley here? That woman in heliotrope, who has just gone out of the room with your brother?

MABEL CHILTERN. Oh, I think Lady Markby brought her. Why do you ask?

LORD GORING. I haven't seen her for years, that is all.

MABEL CHILTERN. What an absurd reason!

LORD GORING. All reasons are absurd.

MABEL CHILTERN. What sort of a woman is she?

LORD GORING. Oh! a genius in the daytime and a beauty at night!

MABEL CHILTERN. I dislike her already.

LORD GORING. That shows your admirable good taste.

VICOMTE DE NANJAC (*approaching*). Ah, the English young lady is the dragon of good taste, is she not? Quite the dragon of good taste.

LORD GORING. So the newspapers are always telling us.

VICOMTE DE NANJAC. I read all your English newspapers, I find them so amusing.

LORD GORING. Then, my dear Nanjac, you must certainly read between the lines.

VICOMTE DE NANJAC. I should like to, but my professor objects. (*To* MABEL CHILTERN.) May I have the pleasure of escorting you to the music-room, Mademoiselle?

MABEL CHILTERN (*looking very disappointed*). Delighted, Vicomte, quite delighted! (*Turning to* LORD GORING.) Aren't you coming to the music-room?

LORD GORING. Not if there is any music going on, Miss Mabel.

MABEL CHILTERN (*severely*). The music is in German. You would not understand it.

Goes out with the VICOMTE DE NANJAC. LORD CAVERSHAM *comes up to his son.*

LORD CAVERSHAM. Well, sir! what are you doing here? Wasting your life as usual! You should be in bed, sir. You keep too late hours! I heard of you the other night at Lady Rufford's dancing till four o'clock in the morning!

LORD GORING. Only a quarter to four, father.

LORD CAVERSHAM. Can't make out how you stand London Society. The thing has gone to the dogs, a lot of damned nobodies talking about nothing.

LORD GORING. I love talking about nothing, father. It is the only thing I know anything about.

LORD CAVERSHAM. You seem to me to be living entirely for pleasure.

LORD GORING. What else is there to live for, father? Nothing ages like happiness.

LORD CAVERSHAM. You are heartless, sir, very heartless!

LORD GORING. I hope not, father. Good evening, Lady Basildon!

LADY BASILDON (*arching two pretty eyebrows*). Are you here? I had no idea you ever came to political parties!

LORD GORING. I adore political parties. They are the only place left to us where people don't talk politics.

LADY BASILDON. I delight in talking politics. I talk them all day long. But I can't bear listening to them. I don't know how the unfortunate men in the House stand these long debates.

LORD GORING. By never listening.

LADY BASILDON. Really?

LORD GORING (*in his most serious manner*). Of course. You see, it is a very dangerous thing to listen. If one listens one may be convinced; and a man who allows himself to be convinced by an argument is a thoroughly unreasonable person.

LADY BASILDON. Ah! that accounts for so much in men that I have never understood, and so much in women that their husbands never appreciate in them!

MRS MARCHMONT (*with a sigh*). Our husbands never appreciate anything in us. We have to go to others for that!

LADY BASILDON (*emphatically*). Yes, always to others, have we not?

LORD GORING (*smiling*). And those are the views of the two ladies who are known to have the most admirable husbands in London.

MRS MARCHMONT. That is exactly what we can't stand. My Reginald is quite hopelessly faultless. He is really unendurably so, at times! There is not the smallest element of excitement in knowing him.

LORD GORING. How terrible! Really, the thing should be more widely known!

LADY BASILDON. Basildon is quite as bad; he is as domestic as if he was a bachelor.

MRS MARCHMONT (*pressing* LADY BASILDON's *hand*). My poor Olivia! We have married perfect husbands, and we are well punished for it.

LORD GORING. I should have thought it was the husbands who were punished.

MRS MARCHMONT (*drawing herself up*). Oh dear, no! They are as happy as possible! And as for trusting us, it is tragic how much they trust us.

LADY BASILDON. Perfectly tragic!

LORD GORING. Or comic, Lady Basildon?

LADY BASILDON. Certainly not comic, Lord Goring. How unkind of you to suggest such a thing!

MRS MARCHMONT. I am afraid Lord Goring is in the camp of the enemy, as usual. I saw him talking to that Mrs Cheveley when lie came in.

LORD GORING. Handsome woman, Mrs Cheveley!

LADY BASILDON (*stiffly*). Please don't praise other women in our presence. You might wait for us to do that!

LORD GORING. I did wait.

MRS MARCHMONT. Well, we are not going to praise her. I hear she went to the Opera on Monday night, and told Tommy Rufford at supper that, as far as she could see, London Society was entirely made up of dowdies and dandies.

LORD GORING. She is quite right, too. The men are all dowdies and the women are all dandies, aren't they?

MRS MARCHMONT (*after a pause*). Oh! do you really think that is what Mrs Cheveley meant?

LORD GORING. Of course. And a very sensible remark for Mrs Cheveley to make, too.

Enter MABEL CHILTERN. *She joins the group.*

MABEL CHILTERN. Why are you talking about Mrs Cheveley? Everybody is talking about Mrs Cheveley! Lord Goring says – what did you say, Lord Goring, about Mrs Cheveley? Oh! I remember, that she was a genius in the daytime and a beauty at night.

LADY BASILDON. What a horrid combination! So very unnatural!

MRS MARCHMONT (*in her most dreamy manner*). I like looking at geniuses, and listening to beautiful people.

LORD GORING. Ah! that is morbid of you, Mrs Marchmont!

MRS MARCHMONT (*brightening to a look of real pleasure*). I am so glad to hear you say that. Marchmont and I have been married for seven years, and he has never once told me that I was morbid. Men are so painfully unobservant!

LADY BASILDON (*turning to her*). I have always said, dear Margaret, that you were the most morbid person in. London.

MRS MARCHMONT. Ah! but you are always sympathetic, Olivia!

MABEL CHILTERN. Is it morbid to have a desire for food? I have a great desire for food. Lord Goring, will you give me some supper?

LORD GORING. With pleasure, Miss Mabel.

Moves away with her.

MABEL CHILTERN. How horrid you have been! You have never talked to me the whole evening!

LORD GORING. How could I? You went away with the child-diplomatist.

MABEL CHILTERN. You might have followed us. Pursuit would have been only polite. I don't think I like you at all this evening!

LORD GORING. I like you immensely.

MABEL CHILTERN. Well, I wish you'd show it in a more marked way!

They go downstairs.

MRS MARCHMONT. Olivia, I have a curious feeling of absolute faintness. I think I should like some supper very much. I know I should like some supper.

LADY BASILDON. I am positively dying for supper, Margaret!

MRS MARCHMONT. Men are so horribly selfish, they never think of these things.

LADY BASILDON. Men are grossly material, grossly material!

The VICOMTE DE NANJAC *enters from the music-room with some other guests. After having carefully examined all the people present, he approaches* LADY BASILDON.

VICOMTE DE NANJAC. May I have the honour of taking you down to supper, Comtesse?

LADY BASILDON (*coldly*). I never take supper, thank you, Vicomte. (*The* VICOMTE *is about to retire.* LADY BASILDON, *seeing this, rises at once and takes his arm.*) But I will come down with you with pleasure.

VICOMTE DE NANJAC. I am so fond of eating! I am very English in all my tastes.

LADY BASILDON. You look quite English, Vicomte, quite English.

They pass out. MR MONTFORD, *a perfectly groomed young dandy, approaches* MRS MARCHMONT.

MR MONTFORD. Like some supper, Mrs Marchmont?

MRS MARCHMONT (*languidly*). Thank you, Mr Montford, I never touch supper. (*Rises hastily and takes his arm.*) But I will sit beside you, and watch you.

MR MONTFORD. I don't know that I like being watched when I am eating!

MRS MARCHMONT. Then I will watch someone else.

MR MONTFORD. I don't know that I should like that either.

MRS MARCHMONT (*severely*). Pray, Mr Montford, do not make these painful scenes of jealousy in public!

They go downstairs with the other guests, passing SIR ROBERT CHILTERN *and* MRS CHEVELEY, *who now enter.*

SIR ROBERT CHILTERN. And are you going to any of our country houses before you leave England, Mrs Cheveley?

MRS CHEVELEY. Oh, no! I can't stand your English house-parties. In England people actually try to be brilliant at breakfast. That is so dreadful of them! Only dull people are brilliant at breakfast. And then the family skeleton is always reading family prayers. My stay in England really depends on you, Sir Robert.

Sits down on the sofa.

SIR ROBERT CHILTERN (*taking a seat beside her*). Seriously?

MRS CHEVELEY. Quite seriously. I want to talk to you about a great political and financial scheme, about this Argentine Canal Company, in fact.

SIR ROBERT CHILTERN. What a tedious, practical subject for you to talk about, Mrs Cheveley!

MRS CHEVELEY. Oh, I like tedious, practical subjects. What I don't like are tedious, practical people. There is a wide difference. Besides, you are interested, I know, in International Canal schemes. You were Lord Radley's secretary, weren't you, when the Government bought the Suez Canal shares?

SIR ROBERT CHILTERN. Yes. But the Suez Canal was a very great and splendid undertaking. It gave us our direct route to India. It had imperial value. It was necessary that we should have control. This Argentine scheme is a commonplace Stock Exchange swindle.

MRS CHEVELEY. A speculation, Sir Robert! A brilliant, daring speculation.

SIR ROBERT CHILTERN. Believe me, Mrs Cheveley, it is a swindle. Let us call things by their proper names. It makes matters simpler. We have all the information about it at the Foreign Office. In fact, I sent out a special Commission to inquire into the matter privately, and they report that the works are hardly begun, and as for the money already subscribed, no one seems to know what has become of it. The whole thing is a second Panama, and with not a quarter of the chance of success that miserable affair ever had. I hope you have not invested in it. I am sure you are far too clever to have done that.

MRS CHEVELEY. I have invested very largely in it.

SIR ROBERT CHILTERN. Who could have advised you to do such a foolish thing?

MRS CHEVELEY. Your old friend – and mine.

SIR ROBERT CHILTERN. Who?

MRS CHEVELEY. Baron Arnheim.

SIR ROBERT CHILTERN (*frowning*). Ah! yes. I remember hearing, at the time of his death, that he had been mixed up in the whole affair.

MRS CHEVELEY. It was his last romance. His last but one, to do him justice.

SIR ROBERT CHILTERN (*rising*). But you have not seen my Corots yet. They are in the music-room. Corots seem to go with music, don't they? May I show them to you?

MRS CHEVELEY (*shaking her head*). I am not in a mood tonight for silver twilights, or rose-pink dawns. I want to talk business.

Motions to him with her fan to sit down again beside her.

SIR ROBERT CHILTERN. I fear I have no advice to give you, Mrs Cheveley, except to interest yourself in something less dangerous. The success of the Canal depends, of course, on the attitude of England, and I am going to lay the report of the Commissioners before the House tomorrow night.

MRS CHEVELEY. That you must not do. In your own interests, Sir Robert, to say nothing of mine, you must not do that.

SIR ROBERT CHILTERN (*looking at her in wonder*). In my own interests? My dear Mrs Cheveley, what do you mean?

Sits down beside her.

MRS CHEVELEY. Sir Robert, I will be quite frank with you. I want you to withdraw the report that you had intended to lay before the House, on the ground that you have reasons to believe that the Commissioners have been prejudiced or misinformed, or something. Then I want you to say a few words to the effect that the Government is going to reconsider the question, and that you have reason to believe that the Canal, if completed, will be of great international value. You know the sort of things ministers say in cases of this kind. A few ordinary platitudes will do. In modern life nothing produces such an effect as a good platitude. It makes the whole world kin. Will you do that for me?

SIR ROBERT CHILTERN. Mrs Cheveley, you cannot be serious in making me such a proposition!

MRS CHEVELEY. I am quite serious.

SIR ROBERT CHILTERN (*coldly*). Pray allow me to believe that you are not.

MRS CHEVELEY (*speaking with great deliberation and emphasis*). Ah! but I am. And if you do what I ask you, I . . . will pay you very handsomely!

SIR ROBERT CHILTERN. Pay me!

MRS CHEVELEY. Yes.

SIR ROBERT CHILTERN. I am afraid I don't quite understand what you mean.

MRS CHEVELEY (*leaning back on the sofa and looking at him*). How very disappointing! And I have come all the way from Vienna in order that you should thoroughly understand me.

SIR ROBERT CHILTERN. I fear I don't.

MRS CHEVELEY (*in her most nonchalant manner*). My dear Sir Robert, you are a man of the world, and you have your price, I suppose. Everybody has nowadays. The drawback is that most people are so dreadfully expensive. I know I am. I hope you will be more reasonable in your terms.

SIR ROBERT CHILTERN (*rises indignantly*). If you will allow me, I will call your carriage for you. You have lived so long abroad, Mrs Cheveley, that you seem to be unable to realise that you are talking to an English gentleman.

MRS CHEVELEY (*detains him by touching his arm with her fan, and keeping it there while she is talking*). I realise that I am talking to a man who laid the foundation of his fortune by selling to a Stock Exchange speculator a Cabinet secret.

SIR ROBERT CHILTERN (*biting his lip*). What do you mean?

MRS CHEVELEY (*rising and facing him*). I mean that I know the real origin of your wealth and your career, and I have got your letter, too.

SIR ROBERT CHILTERN. What letter?

MRS CHEVELEY (*contemptuously*). The letter you wrote to Baron Arnheim, when you were Lord Radley's secretary, telling the Baron to buy Suez Canal shares – a letter written three days before the Government announced its own purchase.

SIR ROBERT CHILTERN (*hoarsely*). It is not true.

MRS CHEVELEY. You thought that letter had been destroyed. How foolish of you! It is in my possession.

SIR ROBERT CHILTERN. The affair to which you allude was no more than a speculation. The House of Commons had not yet passed the bill; it might have been rejected.

MRS CHEVELEY. It was a swindle, Sir Robert. Let us call things by their proper names. It makes everything simpler. And now I am going to sell you that letter, and the price I ask for it is your public support of the Argentine scheme. You made your own fortune out of one canal. You must help me and my friends to make our fortunes out of another!

SIR ROBERT CHILTERN. It is infamous, what you propose – infamous!

MRS CHEVELEY. Oh, no! This is the game of life as we all have to play it, Sir Robert, sooner or later!

SIR ROBERT CHILTERN. I cannot do what you ask me.

MRS CHEVELEY. You mean you cannot help doing it. You know you are standing on the edge of a precipice. And it is not for you to make terms. It is for you to accept them. Supposing you refuse –

SIR ROBERT CHILTERN. What then?

MRS CHEVELEY. My dear Sir Robert, what then? You are ruined, that is all! Remember to what a point your Puritanism in England has brought you. In old days nobody pretended to be a bit better than his neighbours. In fact, to be a bit better than one's neighbour was considered excessively vulgar and middle-class. Nowadays, with our modern mania for morality, everyone has to pose as a paragon of purity, incorruptibility, and all the other seven deadly virtues – and what is the result? You all go over like ninepins – one after the other. Not a year passes in England without somebody disappearing. Scandals used to lend charm, or at least interest, to a man – now they crush him. And yours is a very nasty scandal. You couldn't survive it. If it were known that as a young man, secretary to a great and important minister, you sold a Cabinet secret for a large sum of money, and that that was the origin of your wealth and career, you would be hounded out of public life, you would disappear completely. And after all, Sir Robert, why should you sacrifice your entire future rather than deal diplomatically with your enemy? For the moment I am your enemy. I admit it! And I am much stronger than you are. The big battalions are on my side. You have a splendid position, but it is your splendid position that makes you so vulnerable. You can't defend it! And I am in attack. Of course I have not talked morality to you. You must admit in fairness that I have spared you that. Years ago you did a clever, unscrupulous thing; it turned out a great success. You owe to it your fortune and position. And now you have got to pay for it. Sooner or later we have all to pay for what we do. You have to pay now. Before I leave you tonight, you have got to promise me to suppress your report, and to speak in the House in favour of this scheme.

SIR ROBERT CHILTERN. What you ask is impossible.

MRS CHEVELEY. You must make it possible. You are going to make it possible. Sir Robert, you know what your English newspapers are like. Suppose that when I leave this house I drive down to some newspaper office, and give them this scandal and the proofs of it! Think of their loathsome joy, of the delight they would have in dragging you down, of the mud and mire they would plunge you in. Think of the hypocrite with his greasy smile penning his leading article, and arranging the foulness of the public placard.

SIR ROBERT CHILTERN. Stop! You want me to withdraw the report and to make a short speech stating that I believe there are possibilities in the scheme?

MRS CHEVELEY (*sitting down on the sofa*). Those are my terms.

SIR ROBERT CHILTERN (*in a low voice*). I will give you any sum of money you want.

MRS CHEVELEY. Even you are not rich enough, Sir Robert, to buy back your past. No man is.

SIR ROBERT CHILTERN. I will not do what you ask me. I will not.

MRS CHEVELEY. You have to. If you don't . . .

Rises from the sofa.

SIR ROBERT CHILTERN (*bewildered and unnerved*). Wait a moment! What did you propose? You said that you would give me back my letter, didn't you?

MRS CHEVELEY. Yes. That is agreed. I will be in the Ladies' Gallery tomorrow night at half-past eleven. If by that time – and you will have had heaps of opportunity – you have made an announcement to the House in the terms I wish, I shall hand you back your letter with the prettiest thanks, and the best, or at any rate the most suitable, compliment I can think of. I intend to play quite fairly with you. One should always play fairly . . . when one has the winning cards. The Baron taught me that . . . amongst other things.

SIR ROBERT CHILTERN. You must let me have time to consider your proposal.

MRS CHEVELEY. No; you must settle now!

SIR ROBERT CHILTERN. Give me a week – three days!

MRS CHEVELEY. Impossible! I have got to telegraph to Vienna tonight.

SIR ROBERT CHILTERN. My God! what brought you into my life?

MRS CHEVELEY. Circumstances.

Moves towards the door.

SIR ROBERT CHILTERN. Don't go. I consent. The report shall be withdrawn. I will arrange for a question to be put to me on the subject.

MRS CHEVELEY. Thank you. I knew we should come to an amicable agreement. I understood your nature from the first. I analysed you, though you did not adore me. And now you can get my carriage for me, Sir Robert. I see the people coming up from supper, and English men always get romantic after a meal, and that bores me dreadfully.

Exit SIR ROBERT CHILTERN.

Enter guests, LADY CHILTERN, LADY MARKBY, LORD CAVERSHAM, LADY BASILDON, MRS MARCHMONT, VICOMTE DE NANJAC, MR MONTFORD.

LADY MARKBY. Well, dear Mrs Cheveley, I hope you have enjoyed yourself. Sir Robert is very entertaining, is he not?

MRS CHEVELEY. Most entertaining! I have enjoyed my talk with him immensely.

LADY MARKBY. He has had a very interesting and brilliant career. And he has married a most admirable wife. Lady Chiltern is a woman of the very highest principles, I am glad to say. I am a little too old now, myself, to trouble about setting a good example, but I always admire people who do. And Lady Chiltern has a very ennobling effect on life, though her dinner-parties are rather dull sometimes. But one can't have everything, can one? And now I must go, dear. Shall I call for you tomorrow?

MRS CHEVELEY. Thanks.

LADY MARKBY. We might drive in the Park at five. Everything looks so fresh in the Park now!

MRS CHEVELEY. Except the people!

LADY MARKBY. Perhaps the people are a little jaded. I have often observed that the Season as it goes on produces a kind of softening of the brain. However, I think anything is better than high intellectual pressure. That is the most unbecoming thing there is. It makes the noses of the young girls so particularly large. And there is nothing so difficult to marry as a large nose; men don't like them. Good night, dear! (*To* LADY CHILTERN.) Good night, Gertrude!

Goes out on LORD CAVERSHAM's *arm.*

MRS CHEVELEY. What a charming house you have, Lady Chiltern! I have spent a delightful evening. It has been so interesting getting to know your husband.

LADY CHILTERN. Why did you wish to meet my husband, Mrs Cheveley?

MRS CHEVELEY. Oh, I will tell you. I wanted to interest him in this Argentine Canal scheme, of which I dare say you have heard. And I found him most susceptible, – susceptible to reason, I mean. A rare thing in a man. I converted him in ten minutes. He is going to make a speech in the House tomorrow night in favour of the idea. We must go to the Ladies' Gallery and hear him! It will be a great occasion!

LADY CHILTERN. There must be some mistake. That scheme could never have my husband's support.

MRS CHEVELEY. Oh, I assure you it's all settled. I don't regret my tedious journey from Vienna now. It has been a great success. But, of course, for the next twenty-four hours the whole thing is a dead secret.

LADY CHILTERN (*gently*). A secret? Between whom?

MRS CHEVELEY (*with a flash of amusement in her eyes*). Between your husband and myself.

SIR ROBERT CHILTERN (*entering*). Your carriage is here, Mrs Cheveley!

MRS CHEVELEY. Thanks! Good evening, Lady Chiltern! Good night, Lord Goring! I am at Claridge's. Don't you think you might leave a card?

LORD GORING. If you wish, Mrs Cheveley!

MRS CHEVELEY. Oh, don't be so solemn about it, or I shall be obliged to leave a card on you. In England I suppose that would hardly be considered *en règle*. Abroad, we are more civilised. Will you see me down, Sir Robert? Now that we have both the same interests at heart we shall be great friends, I hope!

Sails out on SIR ROBERT CHILTERN's *arm.* LADY CHILTERN *goes to the top of the staircase and looks down at them as they descend. Her expression is troubled. After a little time she is joined by some of the guests, and passes with them into another reception-room.*

MABEL CHILTERN. What a horrid woman!

LORD GORING. You should go to bed, Miss Mabel.

MABEL CHILTERN. Lord Goring!

LORD GORING. My father told me to go to bed an hour ago. I don't see why I shouldn't give you the same advice. I always pass on good advice. It is the only thing to do with it. It is never of any use to oneself.

MABEL CHILTERN. Lord Goring, you are always ordering me out of the room. I think it most courageous of you. Especially as I am not going to bed for hours. (*Goes over to the sofa.*) You can come and sit down if you like, and talk about anything in the world, except the Royal Academy, Mrs Cheveley, or novels in Scotch dialect. They are not improving subjects. (*Catches sight of something, that is lying on the sofa half hidden by the cushion.*) What is this? Someone has dropped a diamond brooch! Quite beautiful, isn't it? (*Shows it to him.*) I wish it was mine, but Gertrude won't let me wear anything but pearls, and I am thoroughly sick of pearls. They make one look so plain, so good, and so intellectual. I wonder whom the brooch belongs to.

LORD GORING. I wonder who dropped it.

MABEL CHILTERN. It is a beautiful brooch.

LORD GORING. It is a handsome bracelet.

MABEL CHILTERN. It isn't a bracelet. It's a brooch.

LORD GORING. It can be used as a bracelet.

Takes it from her, and, pulling out a green letter-case, puts the ornament carefully in it, and replaces the whole thing in his breast-pocket with the most perfect sang-froid.

MABEL CHILTERN. What are you doing?

LORD GORING. Miss Mabel, I am going to make a rather strange request to you.

MABEL CHILTERN (*eagerly*). Oh, pray do! I have been waiting for it all the evening.

LORD GORING (*is a little taken aback, but recovers himself*). Don't mention to anybody that I have taken charge of this brooch. Should anyone write and claim it, let me know at once.

MABEL CHILTERN. That is a strange request.

LORD GORING. Well, you see I gave this brooch to somebody once, years ago.

MABEL CHILTERN. You did?

LORD GORING. Yes.

LADY CHILTERN enters alone. The other guests have gone.

MABEL CHILTERN. Then I shall certainly bid you good night. Good night, Gertrude!

Exit.

LADY CHILTERN. Good night, dear! (*To* LORD GORING.) You saw whom Lady Markby brought here tonight?

LORD GORING. Yes. It was an unpleasant surprise. What did she come here for?

LADY CHILTERN. Apparently to try and lure Robert to uphold some fraudulent scheme in which she is interested. The Argentine Canal, in fact.

LORD GORING. She has mistaken her man, hasn't she?

LADY CHILTERN. She is incapable of understanding an upright nature like my husband's!

LORD GORING. Yes. I should fancy she came to grief if she tried to get Robert into her toils. It is extraordinary what astounding mistakes clever women make.

LADY CHILTERN. I don't call women of that kind clever. I call them stupid!

LORD GORING. Same thing often. Good night, Lady Chiltern!

LADY CHILTERN. Good night!

Enter SIR ROBERT CHILTERN.

SIR ROBERT CHILTERN. My dear Arthur, you are not going? Do stop a little!

LORD GORING. Afraid I can't, thanks. I have promised to look in at the Hartlocks'. I believe they have got a mauve Hungarian band that plays mauve Hungarian music. See you soon. Good-bye!

Exit.

SIR ROBERT CHILTERN. How beautiful you look tonight, Gertrude!

LADY CHILTERN. Robert, it is not true, is it? You are not going to lend your support to this Argentine speculation? You couldn't!

SIR ROBERT CHILTERN (*starting*). Who told you I intended to do so?

LADY CHILTERN. That woman who has just gone out, Mrs Cheveley, as she calls herself now. She seemed to taunt me with it. Robert, I know this woman. You don't. We were at school together. She was untruthful, dishonest, an evil influence on everyone whose trust or friendship she could win. I hated, I despised her. She stole things, she was a thief. She was sent away for being a thief. Why do you let her influence you?

SIR ROBERT CHILTERN. Gertrude, what you tell me may be true, but it happened many years ago. It is best forgotten! Mrs Cheveley may have changed since then. No one should be entirely judged by their past.

LADY CHILTERN (*sadly*). One's past is what one is. It is the only way by which people should be judged.

SIR ROBERT CHILTERN. That is a hard saying, Gertrude!

LADY CHILTERN. It is a true saying, Robert. And what did she mean by boasting that she had got you to lend your support, your name, to a thing I have heard you describe as the most dishonest and fraudulent scheme there has ever been in political life?

SIR ROBERT CHILTERN (*biting his lip*). I was mistaken in the view I took. We all may make mistakes.

LADY CHILTERN. But you told me yesterday that you had received the report from the Commission, and that it entirely condemned the whole thing.

SIR ROBERT CHILTERN (*walking up and down*). I have reasons now to believe that the Commission was prejudiced, or, at any rate, misinformed. Besides, Gertrude, public and private life are different things. They have different laws, and move on different lines.

LADY CHILTERN. They should both represent man at his highest. I see no difference between them.

SIR ROBERT CHILTERN (*stopping*). In the present case, on a matter of practical politics, I have changed my mind. That is all.

LADY CHILTERN. All!

SIR ROBERT CHILTERN (*sternly*). Yes!

LADY CHILTERN. Robert! Oh! it is horrible that I should have to ask you such a question – Robert, are you telling me the whole truth?

SIR ROBERT CHILTERN. Why do you ask me such a question?

LADY CHILTERN (*after a pause*). Why do you not answer it?

SIR ROBERT CHILTERN (*sitting down*). Gertrude, truth is a very complex thing, and politics is a very complex business. There are wheels within wheels. One may be under certain obligations to people that one must pay. Sooner or later in political life one has to compromise. Everyone does.

LADY CHILTERN. Compromise? Robert, why do you talk so differently tonight from the way I have always heard you talk? Why are you changed?

SIR ROBERT CHILTERN. I am not changed. But circumstances alter things.

LADY CHILTERN. Circumstances should never alter principles!

SIR ROBERT CHILTERN. But if I told you –

LADY CHILTERN. What?

SIR ROBERT CHILTERN. That it was necessary, vitally necessary?

LADY CHILTERN. It can never be necessary to do what is not honourable. Or if it be necessary, then what is it that I have loved! But it is not, Robert; tell me it is not. Why should it be? What gain would you get? Money? We have no need of that! And money that comes from a tainted source is a degradation. Power? But power is nothing in itself. It is power to do good that is fine – that, and that only. What is it, then? Robert, tell me why you are going to do this dishonourable thing!

SIR ROBERT CHILTERN. Gertrude, you have no right to use that word. I told you it was a question of rational compromise. It is no more than that.

LADY CHILTERN. Robert, that is all very well for other men, for men who treat life simply as a sordid speculation; but not for you, Robert, not for you. You are different. All your life you have stood apart from others. You have never let the world soil you. To the world, as to myself, you have been an ideal always. Oh! be that ideal still. That great inheritance throw not away – that tower of ivory do not destroy. Robert, men can love what is beneath them – things unworthy, stained, dishonoured. We women worship when we love; and when we lose our worship, we lose everything. Oh! don't kill my love for you, don't kill that!

SIR ROBERT CHILTERN. Gertrude!

LADY CHILTERN. I know that there are men with horrible secrets in their lives – men who have done some shameful thing, and who in some critical moment have to pay for it, by doing some other act of shame – oh! don't tell me you are such as they are! Robert, is there in your life any secret dishonour or disgrace? Tell me, tell me at once, that –

SIR ROBERT CHILTERN. That what?

LADY CHILTERN (*speaking very slowly*). That our lives may drift apart.

SIR ROBERT CHILTERN. Drift apart?

LADY CHILTERN. That they may be entirely separate. It would be better for us both.

SIR ROBERT CHILTERN. Gertrude, there is nothing in my past life that you might not know.

LADY CHILTERN. I was sure of it, Robert, I was sure of it. But why did you say those dreadful things, things so unlike your real self? Don't let us ever talk about the subject again. You will write, won't you, to Mrs Cheveley, and tell her that you cannot support this scandalous scheme of hers? If you have given her any promise you must take it back, that is all!

SIR ROBERT CHILTERN. Must I write and tell her that?

LADY CHILTERN. Surely, Robert! What else is there to do?

SIR ROBERT CHILTERN. I might see her personally. It would be better.

LADY CHILTERN. You must never see her again, Robert. She is not a woman you should ever speak to. She is not worthy to talk to a man like you. No; you must write to her at once, now, this moment, and let your letter show her that your decision is quite irrevocable!

SIR ROBERT CHILTERN. Write this moment!

LADY CHILTERN. Yes.

SIR ROBERT CHILTERN. But it is so late. It is close on twelve.

LADY CHILTERN. That makes no matter. She must know at once that she has been mistaken in you – and that you are not a man to do anything base or underhand or dishonourable. Write here, Robert. Write that you decline to support this scheme of hers, as you hold it to be a dishonest scheme. Yes – write the word dishonest. She knows what that word means.

SIR ROBERT CHILTERN *sits down and writes a letter. His wife takes it up and reads it.*

Yes; that will do. (*Rings bell.*) And now the envelope. (*He writes the envelope slowly. Enter* MASON.) Have this letter sent at once to Claridge's Hotel. There is no answer. (*Exit* MASON. LADY CHILTERN *kneels down beside her husband and puts her arms around him.*) Robert, love gives one an instinct to things. I feel tonight that I have saved you from something that might have been a danger to you, from something that might have made men honour you less than they do. I don't think you realise sufficiently, Robert, that you have brought into the political life of our time a nobler atmosphere, a finer attitude towards life, a freer air of purer aims and higher ideals – I know it, and for that I love you, Robert.

SIR ROBERT CHILTERN. Oh, love me always, Gertrude, love me always!

LADY CHILTERN. I will love you always, because you will always be worthy of love. We needs must love the highest when we see it!

Kisses him and rises and goes out.

SIR ROBERT CHILTERN *walks up and down for a moment; then sits down and buries his face in his hands. The Servant enters and begins putting out the lights.* SIR ROBERT CHILTERN *looks up.*

SIR ROBERT CHILTERN. Put out the lights, Mason, put out the lights!

The Servant puts out the lights. The room becomes almost dark. The only light there is comes from the great chandelier that hangs over the staircase and illumines the tapestry of the Triumph of Love.

Act drop.

SECOND ACT

Scene: Morning-Room at Sir Robert Chiltern's house.

LORD GORING, *dressed in the height of fashion, is lounging in an armchair,* SIR ROBERT CHILTERN *is standing in front of the fireplace. He is evidently in a state of great mental excitement and distress. As the scene progresses he paces nervously up and down the room.*

LORD GORING. My dear Robert, it's a very awkward business, very awkward indeed. You should have told your wife the whole thing. Secrets from other people's wives are a necessary luxury in modern life. So, at least, I am always told at the club by people who are bald enough to know better. But no man should have a secret from his own wife. She invariably finds it out. Women have a wonderful instinct about things. They can discover everything except the obvious.

SIR ROBERT CHILTERN. Arthur, I couldn't tell my wife. When could I have told her? Not last night. It would have made a lifelong separation between us, and I would have lost the love of the one woman in the world I worship, of the only woman who has ever stirred love within me. Last night it would have been quite impossible. She would have turned from me in horror . . . in horror and in contempt.

LORD GORING. Is Lady Chiltern as perfect as all that?

SIR ROBERT CHILTERN. Yes, my wife is as perfect as all that.

LORD GORING (*taking off his left-hand glove*). What a pity! I beg your pardon, my dear fellow, I didn't quite mean that. But if what you tell me is true, I should like to have a serious talk about life with Lady Chiltern.

SIR ROBERT CHILTERN. It would be quite useless.

LORD GORING. May I try?

SIR ROBERT CHILTERN. Yes; but nothing could make her alter her views.

LORD GORING. Well, at the worst it would simply be a psychological experiment.

SIR ROBERT CHILTERN. All such experiments are terribly dangerous.

LORD GORING. Everything is dangerous, my dear fellow. If it wasn't so, life wouldn't be worth living . . . Well, I am bound to say that I think you should have told her years ago.

SIR ROBERT CHILTERN. When? When we were engaged? Do you think she would have married me if she had known that the origin of my fortune is such as it is, the basis of my career such as it is, and that I had done a thing that I suppose most men would call shameful and dishonourable?

LORD GORING (*slowly*). Yes; most men would call it ugly names. There is no doubt of that.

SIR ROBERT CHILTERN (*bitterly*). Men who every day do something of the same kind themselves. Men who, each one of them, have worse secrets in their own lives.

LORD GORING. That is the reason they are so pleased to find out other people's secrets. It distracts public attention from their own.

SIR ROBERT CHILTERN. And, after all, whom did I wrong by what I did? No one.

LORD GORING (*looking at him steadily*). Except yourself, Robert.

SIR ROBERT CHILTERN (*after a pause*). Of course I had private information about a certain transaction contemplated by the Government of the day, and I acted on it. Private information is practically the source of every large modern fortune.

LORD GORING (*tapping his boot with his cane*). And public scandal invariably the result.

SIR ROBERT CHILTERN (*pacing up and down the room*). Arthur, do you think that what I did nearly eighteen years ago should be brought up against me now? Do you think it fair that a man's whole career should be ruined for a fault done in one's boyhood almost? I was twenty-two at the time, and I had the double misfortune of being well-born and poor, two unforgivable things nowadays. Is it fair that the folly, the sin of one's youth, if men choose to call it a sin, should wreck a life like mine, should place me in the pillory, should shatter all that I have worked for, all that I have built up? Is it fair, Arthur?

LORD GORING. Life is never fair, Robert. And perhaps it is a good thing for most of us that it is not.

SIR ROBERT CHILTERN. Every man of ambition has to fight his century with its own weapons. What this century worships is wealth. The god of this century is wealth. To succeed one must have wealth. At all costs one must have wealth.

LORD GORING. You underrate yourself, Robert. Believe me, without wealth you could have succeeded just as well.

SIR ROBERT CHILTERN. When I was old, perhaps. When I had lost my passion for power, or could not use it. When I was tired, worn out, disappointed. I wanted my success when I was young. Youth is the time for success. I couldn't wait.

LORD GORING. Well, you certainly have had your success while you are still young. No one in our day has had such a brilliant success. Under-Secretary for Foreign Affairs at the age of forty – that's good enough for anyone, I should think.

SIR ROBERT CHILTERN. And if it is all taken away from me now? If I lose everything over a horrible scandal? If I am hounded from public life?

LORD GORING. Robert, how could you have sold yourself for money?

SIR ROBERT CHILTERN (*excitedly*). I did not sell myself for money. I bought success at a great price. That is all.

LORD GORING (*gravely*). Yes; you certainly paid a great price for it. But what first made you think of doing such a thing?

SIR ROBERT CHILTERN. Baron Arnheim.

LORD GORING. Damned scoundrel!

SIR ROBERT CHILTERN. No; he was a man of a most subtle and refined intellect. A man of culture, charm, and distinction. One of the most intellectual men I ever met.

LORD GORING. Ah! I prefer a gentlemanly fool any day. There is more to be said for stupidity than people imagine. Personally I have a great admiration for stupidity. It is a sort of fellow-feeling, I suppose. But how did he do it? Tell me the whole thing.

SIR ROBERT CHILTERN (*throws himself into an armchair by the writing-table*). One night after dinner at Lord Radley's the Baron began talking about success in modern life as something that one could reduce to an absolutely definite science. With that wonderfully fascinating quiet voice of his he expounded to us the most terrible of all philosophies, the philosophy of power, preached to us the most marvellous of all gospels, the gospel of gold. I think he saw the effect he had produced on me, for some days afterwards he wrote and asked me to come and see him. He was living then in Park Lane, in the house Lord Woolcomb has now. I remember so well how, with a strange smile on his pale, curved lips, he led me through his wonderful picture gallery, showed me his tapestries, his enamels, his jewels, his carved ivories, made me wonder at the strange loveliness of the luxury in which he lived; and then told me that luxury was nothing but a background, a painted scene in a play, and that power, power over other men, power over the world, was the one thing worth having, the one supreme pleasure worth knowing, the one joy one never tired of, and that in our century only the rich possessed it.

LORD GORING. (*with great deliberation*). A thoroughly shallow creed.

SIR ROBERT CHILTERN (*rising*). I didn't think so then. I don't think so now. Wealth has given me enormous power. It gave me at the very outset of my life freedom, and freedom is everything. You have never been poor, and never known what ambition is. You cannot understand what a wonderful chance the Baron gave me. Such a chance as few men get.

LORD GORING. Fortunately for them, if one is to judge by results. But tell me definitely, how did the Baron finally persuade you to – well, to do what you did?

SIR ROBERT CHILTERN. When I was going away he said to me that if I ever could give him any private information of real value, he would make me a very rich man. I was dazed at the prospect he held out to me, and my ambition and my desire for power were at that time boundless. Six weeks later certain private documents passed through my hands.

LORD GORING (*keeping his eyes steadily fixed on the carpet*). State documents?

SIR ROBERT CHILTERN. Yes.

LORD GORING *sighs, then passes his hand across his forehead and looks up.*

LORD GORING. I had no idea that you, of all men in the world, could have been so weak, Robert, as to yield to such a temptation as Baron Arnheim held out to you.

SIR ROBERT CHILTERN. Weak? Oh, I am sick of hearing that phrase. Sick of using it about others. Weak? Do you really think, Arthur, that it is weakness that yields to temptation? I tell you that there are terrible temptations that it requires strength, strength and courage, to yield to. To stake all one's life on a single moment, to risk everything on one throw, whether the stake be power or pleasure, I care not – there is no weakness in that. There is a horrible, a terrible courage. I had that courage. I sat down the same afternoon and wrote Baron Arnheim the letter this woman now holds. He made three-quarters of a million over the transaction.

LORD GORING. And you?

SIR ROBERT CHILTERN. I received from the Baron £110,000.

LORD GORING. You were worth more, Robert.

SIR ROBERT CHILTERN. No; that money gave me exactly what I wanted, power over others. I went into the House immediately. The Baron advised me in finance from time to time. Before five years I had almost trebled my fortune. Since then everything that I have touched has turned out a success. In all things connected with money I have had a luck so extraordinary that sometimes it has made me almost afraid. I remember having read somewhere, in some strange book, that when the gods wish to punish us they answer our prayers.

LORD GORING. But tell me, Robert, did you ever suffer any regret for what you had done?

SIR ROBERT CHILTERN. No. I felt that I had fought the century with its own weapons, and won.

LORD GORING (*sadly*). You thought you had won.

SIR ROBERT CHILTERN. I thought so. (*After a long pause.*) Arthur, do you despise me for what I have told you?

LORD GORING (*with deep feeling in his voice*). I am very sorry for you, Robert, very sorry indeed,

SIR ROBERT CHILTERN. I don't say that I suffered any remorse. I didn't. Not remorse in the ordinary, rather silly sense of the word. But I have paid conscience money many times. I had a wild hope that I might disarm destiny. The sum Baron Arnheim gave me I have distributed twice over in public charities since then.

LORD GORING (*looking up*). In public charities? Dear me! what a lot of harm you must have done, Robert!

SIR ROBERT CHILTERN. Oh, don't say that, Arthur; don't talk like that!

LORD GORING. Never mind what I say, Robert! I am always saying what I shouldn't say. In fact, I usually say what I really think. A great mistake nowadays. It makes one so liable to be misunderstood. As regards this dreadful business, I will help you in whatever way I can. Of course, you know that.

SIR ROBERT CHILTERN. Thank you, Arthur, thank you. But what is to be done? What can be done?

LORD GORING (*leaning back with his hands in his pockets*). Well, the English can't stand a man who is always saying he is in the right, but they are very fond of a man who admits that he has been in the wrong. It is one of the best things in them. However, in your case, Robert, a confession would not do. The money, if you will allow me to say so, is . . . awkward. Besides, if you did make a clean breast of the whole affair, you would never be able to talk morality again. And in England a man who can't talk morality twice a week to a large, popular, immoral audience is quite over as a serious politician. There would be nothing left for him as a profession except Botany or the Church. A confession would be of no use. It would ruin you.

SIR ROBERT CHILTERN. It would ruin me. Arthur, the only thing for me to do now is to fight the thing out.

LORD GORING (*rising from his chair*). I was waiting for you to say that, Robert. It is the only thing to do now. And you must begin by telling your wife the whole story.

SIR ROBERT CHILTERN. That I will not do.

LORD GORING. Robert, believe me, you are wrong.

SIR ROBERT CHILTERN. I couldn't do it. It would kill her love for me. And now about this woman, this Mrs Cheveley. How can I defend myself against her? You knew her before, Arthur, apparently.

LORD GORING. Yes.

SIR ROBERT CHILTERN. Did you know her well?

LORD GORING (*arranging his necktie*). So little that I got engaged to be married to her once, when I was staying at the Tenbys'. The affair lasted for three days . . . nearly.

SIR ROBERT CHILTERN. Why was it broken off?

LORD GORING (*airily*). Oh, I forget. At least, it makes no matter. By the way, have you tried her with money? She used to be confoundedly fond of money.

SIR ROBERT CHILTERN. I offered her any sum she wanted. She refused.

LORD GORING. Then the marvellous gospel of gold breaks down sometimes. The rich can't do everything, after all.

SIR ROBERT CHILTERN. Not everything. I suppose you are right. Arthur, I feel that public disgrace is in store for me.

I feel certain of it. I never knew what terror was before. I know it now. It is as if a hand of ice were laid upon one's heart. It is as if one's heart were beating itself to death in some empty hollow.

LORD GORING (*striking the table*). Robert, you must fight her. You must fight her.

SIR ROBERT CHILTERN. But how?

LORD GORING. I can't tell you how at present. I have not the smallest idea. But everyone has some weak point. There is some flaw in each one of us. (*Strolls over to the fireplace and looks at himself in the glass.*) My father tells me that even I have faults. Perhaps I have. I don't know.

SIR ROBERT CHILTERN. In defending myself against Mrs Cheveley, I have a right to use any weapon I can find, have I not?

LORD GORING (*still looking in the glass*). In your place I don't think I should have the smallest scruple in doing so. She is thoroughly well able to take care of herself.

SIR ROBERT CHILTERN (*sits down at the table and takes a pen in his hand*). Well, I shall send a cipher telegram to the Embassy at Vienna to inquire if there is anything known against her. There may be some secret scandal she might be afraid of.

LORD GORING (*settling his buttonhole*). Oh, I should fancy Mrs Cheveley is one of those very modern women of our time who find a new scandal as becoming as a new bonnet, and air them both in the Park every afternoon at five-thirty. I am sure she adores scandals, and that the sorrow of her life at present is that she can't manage to have enough of them.

SIR ROBERT CHILTERN (*writing*). Why do you say that?

LORD GORING (*turning round*). Well, she wore far too much rouge last night, and not quite enough clothes. That is always a sign of despair in a woman.

SIR ROBERT CHILTERN (*striking a bell*). But it is worth while my wiring to Vienna, is it not?

LORD GORING. It is always worth while asking a question, though it is not always worth while answering one.

Enter MASON.

SIR ROBERT CHILTERN. Is Mr Trafford in his room?

MASON. Yes, Sir Robert.

SIR ROBERT CHILTERN (*puts what he has written into an envelope, which he then carefully closes*). Tell him to have this sent off in cipher at once. There must not be a moment's delay.

MASON. Yes, Sir Robert.

SIR ROBERT CHILTERN. Oh! just give that back to me again.

Writes something on the envelope. MASON *then goes out with the letter.*

SIR ROBERT CHILTERN. She must have had some curious hold over Baron Arnheim. I wonder what it was.

LORD GORING (*smiling*). I wonder.

SIR ROBERT CHILTERN. I will fight her to the death, as long as my wife knows nothing.

LORD GORING (*strongly*). Oh, fight in any case – in any case.

SIR ROBERT CHILTERN (*with a gesture of despair*). If my wife found out, there would be little left to fight for. Well, as soon as I hear from Vienna, I shall let you know the result. It is a chance, just a chance, but I believe in it. And as I fought the age with its weapons, I will fight her with her weapons. It is only fair, and she looks like a woman with a past, doesn't she?

LORD GORING. Most pretty women do. But there is a fashion in pasts just as there is a fashion in frocks. Perhaps Mrs Cheveley's past is merely a slight *décolleté* one, and they are excessively popular nowadays. Besides, my dear Robert, I should not build too high hopes on frightening Mrs Cheveley. I should not fancy Mrs Cheveley is a woman who would be easily frightened. She has survived all her creditors, and she shows wonderful presence of mind.

SIR ROBERT CHILTERN. Oh! I live on hopes now. I clutch at every chance. I feel like a man on a ship that is sinking. The water is round my feet, and the very air is bitter with storm. Hush! I hear my wife's voice.

Enter LADY CHILTERN *in walking dress.*

LADY CHILTERN. Good afternoon, Lord Goring!

LORD GORING. Good afternoon, Lady Chiltern! Have you been in the Park?

LADY CHILTERN. No; I have just come from the Woman's Liberal Association, where, by the way, Robert, your name was received with loud applause, and now I have come in to have my tea. (*To* LORD GORING.) You will wait and have some tea, won't you?

LORD GORING. I'll wait for a short time, thanks.

LADY CHILTERN. I will be back in a moment. I am only going to take my hat off.

LORD GORING. (*in his most earnest manner*). Oh! please don't. It is so pretty. One of the prettiest hats I ever saw. I hope the Woman's Liberal Association received it with loud applause.

LADY CHILTERN (*with a smile*). We have much more important work to do than look at each other's bonnets, Lord Goring.

LORD GORING. Really? What sort of work?

LADY CHILTERN. Oh! dull, useful, delightful things, Factory Acts, Female Inspectors, the Eight Hours' Bill, the Parliamentary Franchise. . . . Everything, in fact, that you would find thoroughly uninteresting.

LORD GORING. And never bonnets?

LADY CHILTERN (*with mock indignation*). Never bonnets, never!

LADY CHILTERN *goes through the door leading to her boudoir.*

SIR ROBERT CHILTERN (*takes* LORD GORING's *hand*). You have been a good friend to me, Arthur, a thoroughly good friend.

LORD GORING. I don't know that I have been able to do much for you, Robert, as yet. In fact, I have not been able to do anything for you, as far as I can see. I am thoroughly disappointed with myself.

SIR ROBERT CHILTERN. You have enabled me to tell you the truth. That is something. The truth has always stifled me.

LORD GORING. Ah! the truth is a thing I get rid of as soon as possible! Bad habit, by the way. Makes one very unpopular at the club . . . with the older members. They call it being conceited. Perhaps it is.

SIR ROBERT CHILTERN. I would to God that I had been able to tell the truth . . . to live the truth. Ah! that is the great thing in life, to live the truth. (*Sighs, and goes towards the door.*) I'll see you soon again, Arthur, shan't I?

LORD GORING. Certainly. Whenever you like. I'm going to look in at the Bachelors' Ball tonight, unless I find something better to do. But I'll come round tomorrow morning. If you should want me tonight by any chance, send round a note to Curzon Street.

SIR ROBERT CHILTERN. Thank you.

As he reaches the door, LADY CHILTERN *enters from her boudoir.*

LADY CHILTERN. You are not going, Robert?

SIR ROBERT CHILTERN. I have some letters to write, dear.

LADY CHILTERN (*going to him*). You work too hard, Robert. You seem never to think of yourself, and you are looking so tired.

SIR ROBERT CHILTERN. It is nothing, dear, nothing.

He kisses her and goes out.

LADY CHILTERN (*to* LORD GORING). Do sit down. I am so glad you have called. I want to talk to you about . . . well, not about bonnets, or the Woman's Liberal Association. You take far too much interest in the first subject, and not nearly enough in the second.

LORD GORING. You want to talk to me about Mrs Cheveley?

LADY CHILTERN. Yes. You have guessed it. After you left last night I found out that what she had said was really true. Of course I made Robert write her a letter at once, withdrawing his promise.

LORD GORING. So he gave me to understand.

LADY CHILTERN. To have kept it would have been the first stain on a career that has been stainless always. Robert must be above reproach. He is not like other men. He cannot afford to do what other men do. (*She looks at* LORD GORING, *who remains silent.*) Don't you agree with me? You are Robert's greatest friend. You are our greatest friend, Lord Goring. No one, except myself, knows Robert better than you do. He has no secrets from me, and I don't think he has any from you.

LORD GORING. He certainly has no secrets from me. At least I don't think so.

LADY CHILTERN. Then am I not right in my estimate of him? I know I am right. But speak to me frankly.

LORD GORING (*looking straight at her*). Quite frankly?

LADY CHILTERN. Surely. You have nothing to conceal have you?

LORD GORING. Nothing. But, my dear Lady Chiltern, I think, if you will allow me to say so, that in practical life –

LADY CHILTERN (*smiling*). Of which you know so little, Lord Goring –

LORD GORING. Of which I know nothing by experience, though I know something by observation. I think that in practical life there is something about success, actual success, that is a little unscrupulous, something about ambition that is unscrupulous always. Once a man has set his heart and soul on getting to a certain point, if he has to climb the crag, he climbs the crag; if he has to walk in the mire –

LADY CHILTERN. Well?

LORD GORING. He walks in the mire. Of course I am only talking generally about life.

LADY CHILTERN (*gravely*). I hope so. Why do you look at me so strangely, Lord Goring?

LORD GORING. Lady Chiltern, I have sometimes thought that . . . perhaps you are a little hard in some of your views on life. I think that . . . often you don't make sufficient allowances. In every nature there are elements of weakness, or worse than weakness. Supposing, for instance, that – that any public man, my father, or Lord Merton, or Robert, say, had, years ago, written some foolish letter to someone . . .

LADY CHILTERN. What do you mean by a foolish letter?

LORD GORING. A letter gravely compromising one's position. I am only putting an imaginary case.

LADY CHILTERN. Robert is as incapable of doing a foolish thing as he is of doing a wrong thing.

LORD GORING (*after a long pause*). Nobody is incapable of doing a foolish thing. Nobody is incapable of doing a wrong thing.

LADY CHILTERN. Are you a Pessimist? What will the other dandies say? They will all have to go into mourning.

LORD GORING (*rising*). No, Lady Chiltern, I am not a Pessimist. Indeed I am not sure that I quite know what Pessimism really means. All I do know is that life cannot be understood without much charity, cannot be lived without much charity. It is love, and not German philosophy, that is the true explanation of this world, whatever may be the explanation of the next. And if you are ever in trouble, Lady Chiltern, trust me absolutely, and I will help you in every way I can. If you ever want me, come to me for my assistance, and you shall have it. Come at once to me.

LADY CHILTERN (*looking at him in surprise*). Lord Goring, you are talking quite seriously. I don't think I ever heard you talk seriously before.

LORD GORING (*laughing*). You must excuse me, Lady Chiltern. It won't occur again, if I can help it.

LADY CHILTERN. But I like you to be serious.

Enter MABEL CHILTERN, *in the most ravishing frock.*

MABEL CHILTERN. Dear Gertrude, don't say such a dreadful thing to Lord Goring. Seriousness would be very unbecoming to him. Good afternoon, Lord Goring! Pray be as trivial as you can.

LORD GORING. I should like to, Miss Mabel, but I am afraid I am . . . a little out of practice this morning; and besides, I have to be going now.

MABEL CHILTERN. Just when I have come in! What dreadful manners you have! I am sure you were very badly brought up.

LORD GORING. I was.

MABEL CHILTERN. I wish I had brought you up!

LORD GORING. I am so sorry you didn't.

MABEL CHILTERN. It is too late now, I suppose?

LORD GORING (*smiling*). I am not so sure.

MABEL CHILTERN. Will you ride tomorrow morning?

LORD GORING. Yes, at ten.

MABEL CHILTERN. Don't forget.

LORD GORING. Of course I shan't. By the way, Lady Chiltern, there is no list of your guests in *The Morning Post* of today. It has apparently been crowded out by the County Council, or the Lambeth Conference, or something equally boring. Could you let me have a list? I have a particular reason for asking you.

LADY CHILTERN. I am sure Mr Trafford will be able to give you one.

LORD GORING. Thanks, so much.

MABEL CHILTERN. Tommy is the most useful person in London.

LORD GORING (*turning to her*). And who is the most ornamental?

MABEL CHILTERN (*triumphantly*). I am.

LORD GORING. How clever of you to guess it! (*Takes up his hat and cane.*) Good-bye, Lady Chiltern! You will remember what I said to you, won't you?

LADY CHILTERN. Yes; but I don't know why you said it to me.

LORD GORING. I hardly know myself. Good-bye, Miss Mabel!

MABEL CHILTERN (*with a little moue of disappointment*). I wish you were not going. I have had four wonderful adventures this morning; four and a half, in fact. You might stop and listen to some of them.

LORD GORING. How very selfish of you to have four and a half! There won't be any left for me.

MABEL CHILTERN. I don't want you to have any. They would not be good for you.

LORD GORING. That is the first unkind thing you have ever said to me. How charmingly you said it! Ten tomorrow.

MABEL CHILTERN. Sharp.

LORD GORING. Quite sharp. But don't bring Mr Trafford.

MABEL CHILTERN (*with a little toss of the head*). Of course I shan't bring Tommy Trafford. Tommy Trafford is in great disgrace.

LORD GORING. I am delighted to hear it.

Bows and goes out.

MABEL CHILTERN. Gertrude, I wish you would speak to Tommy Trafford.

LADY CHILTERN. What has poor Mr Trafford done this time? Robert says he is the best secretary he has ever had.

MABEL CHILTERN. Well, Tommy has proposed to me again. Tommy really does nothing but propose to me. He proposed to me last night in the music-room, when I was quite unprotected, as there was an elaborate trio going on. I didn't dare to make the smallest repartee, I need hardly tell you. If I had, it would have stopped the music at once. Musical people are so absurdly unreasonable. They always want one to be perfectly dumb at the very moment when one is longing to be absolutely deaf. Then he proposed to me in broad daylight this morning, in front of that dreadful statue of Achilles. Really, the things that go on in front of that work of art are quite appalling. The police should interfere. At luncheon I saw by the glare in his eye that he was going to propose again, and I just managed to check him in time by assuring him that I was a bimetallist. Fortunately I don't know what bimetallism means. And I don't believe anybody else does either. But the observation crushed Tommy for ten minutes. He looked quite shocked. And then Tommy is so annoying in the way he proposes. If he proposed at the top of his voice, I should not mind so much. That might produce some effect on the public. But he does it in a horrid confidential way. When Tommy wants to be romantic he talks to one just like a doctor. I am very fond of Tommy, but his methods of proposing are quite out of date. I wish, Gertrude, you would speak to him, and tell him that once a week is quite often enough to propose to any one, and that it should always be done in a manner that attracts some attention.

LADY CHILTERN. Dear Mabel, don't talk like that. Besides, Robert thinks very highly of Mr Trafford. He believes he has a brilliant future before him.

MABEL CHILTERN. Oh! I wouldn't marry a man with a future before him for anything under the sun.

LADY CHILTERN. Mabel!

MABEL CHILTERN. I know, dear. You married a man with a future, didn't you? But then Robert was a genius, and you have a noble, self-sacrificing character. You can stand geniuses. I have no character at all, and Robert is the only genius I could ever bear. As a rule, I think they are quite impossible. Geniuses talk so much, don't they? Such a bad habit! And they are always thinking about themselves, when I want them to be thinking about me. I must go round now and rehearse at Lady Basildon's. You remember, we are having tableaux, don't you? The Triumph of something, I don't know what! I hope it will be triumph of me. Only triumph I am really interested in at present. (*Kisses* LADY CHILTERN *and goes out; then comes running back.*) Oh, Gertrude, do you know who is coming to see you? That dreadful Mrs Cheveley, in a most lovely gown. Did you ask her?

LADY CHILTERN (*rising*). Mrs Cheveley! Coming to see me? Impossible!

MABEL CHILTERN. I assure you she is coming upstairs, as large as life and not nearly so natural.

LADY CHILTERN. You need not wait, Mabel. Remember, Lady Basildon is expecting you.

MABEL CHILTERN. Oh! I must shake hands with Lady Markby. She is delightful. I love being scolded by her.

Enter MASON.

MASON. Lady Markby. Mrs Cheveley.

Enter LADY MARKBY *and* MRS CHEVELEY.

LADY CHILTERN (*advancing to meet them*). Dear Lady Markby, how nice of you to come and see me! (*Shakes hands with her, and bows somewhat distantly to* MRS CHEVELEY.) Won't you sit down, Mrs Cheveley?

MRS CHEVELEY. Thanks. Isn't that Miss Chiltern? I should like so much to know her.

LADY CHILTERN. Mabel, Mrs Cheveley wishes to know you.

MABEL CHILTERN *gives a little nod.*

MRS CHEVELEY (*sitting down*). I thought your frock so charming last night, Miss Chiltern. So simple and . . . suitable.

MABEL CHILTERN. Really? I must tell my dressmaker. It will be such a surprise to her. Good-bye, Lady Markby!

LADY MARKBY. Going already?

MABEL CHILTERN. I am so sorry but I am obliged to. I am just off to rehearsal. I have got to stand on my head in some tableaux.

LADY MARKBY. On your head, child? Oh! I hope not. I believe it is most unhealthy.

Takes a seat on the sofa next LADY CHILTERN.

MABEL CHILTERN. But it is for an excellent charity: in aid of the Undeserving, the only people I am really interested in. I am the secretary, and Tommy Trafford is treasurer.

MRS CHEVELEY. And what is Lord Goring?

MABEL CHILTERN. Oh! Lord Goring is president.

MRS CHEVELEY. The post should suit him admirably, unless he has deteriorated since I knew him first.

LADY MARKBY (*reflecting*). You are remarkably modern, Mabel. A little too modern, perhaps. Nothing is so dangerous as being too modern. One is apt to grow old-fashioned quite suddenly. I have known many instances of it.

MABEL CHILTERN. What a dreadful prospect!

LADY MARKBY. Ah! my dear, you need not be nervous. You will always be as pretty as possible. That is the best fashion there is, and the only fashion that England succeeds in setting.

MABEL CHILTERN (*with a curtsey*). Thank you so much, Lady Markby, for England . . . and myself.

Goes out.

LADY MARKBY (*turning to* LADY CHILTERN). Dear Gertrude, we just called to know if Mrs Cheveley's diamond brooch has been found.

LADY CHILTERN. Here?

MRS CHEVELEY. Yes. I missed it when I got back to Claridge's, and I thought I might possibly have dropped it here.

LADY CHILTERN. I have heard nothing about it. But I will send for the butler and ask.

Touches the bell.

MRS CHEVELEY. Oh, pray don't trouble, Lady Chiltern. I dare say I lost it at the Opera, before we came on here.

LADY MARKBY. Ah yes, I suppose it must have been at the Opera. The fact is, we all scramble and jostle so much nowadays that I wonder we have anything at all left on us at the end of an evening. I know myself that, when I am coming back from the Drawing Room, I always feel as if I hadn't a shred on me, except a small shred of decent reputation, just enough to prevent the lower classes making

painful observations through the windows of the carriage.
The fact is that our Society is terribly over-populated.
Really, someone should arrange a proper scheme of assisted
emigration. It would do a great deal of good.

MRS CHEVELEY. I quite agree with you, Lady Markby. It is
nearly six years since I have been in London for the Season,
and I must say Society has become dreadfully mixed. One
sees the oddest people everywhere.

LADY MARKBY. That is quite true, dear. But one needn't
know them. I'm sure I don't know half the people who come
to my house. Indeed, from all I hear, I shouldn't like to.

Enter MASON.

LADY CHILTERN. What sort of a brooch was it that you lost,
Mrs Cheveley?

MRS CHEVELEY. A diamond snake-brooch with a ruby, a
rather large ruby.

LADY MARKBY. I thought you said there was a sapphire on
the head, dear?

MRS CHEVELEY (*smiling*). No, Lady Markby – a ruby.

LADY MARKBY (*nodding her head*). And very becoming, I am
quite sure.

LADY CHILTERN. Has a ruby and diamond brooch been
found in any of the rooms this morning, Mason?

MASON. No, my lady.

MRS CHEVELEY. It really is of no consequence, Lady Chiltern.
I am so sorry to have put you to any inconvenience.

LADY CHILTERN (*coldly*). Oh, it has been no inconvenience.
That will do, Mason. You can bring tea.

Exit MASON.

LADY MARKBY. Well, I must say it is most annoying to lose
anything. I remember once at Bath, years ago, losing in the
Pump Room an exceedingly handsome cameo bracelet that
Sir John had given me. I don't think he has ever given me
anything since, I am sorry to say. He has sadly degenerated.

Really, this horrid House of Commons quite ruins our husbands for us. I think the Lower House by far the greatest blow to a happy married life that there has been since that terrible thing called the Higher Education of Women was invented.

LADY CHILTERN. Ah! it is heresy to say that in this house, Lady Markby. Robert is a great champion of the Higher Education of Women, and so, I am afraid, am I.

MRS CHEVELEY. The higher education of men is what I should like to see. Men need it so sadly.

LADY MARKBY. They do, dear. But I am afraid such a scheme would be quite impractical. I don't think man has much capacity for development. He has got as far as he can, and that is not far, is it? With regard to women, well, dear Gertrude, you belong to the younger generation, and I am sure it is all right if you approve of it. In my time, of course, we were taught not to understand anything. That was the old system, and wonderfully interesting it was. I assure you that the amount of things I and my poor dear sister were taught not to understand was quite extraordinary. But modern women understand everything, I am told.

MRS CHEVELEY. Except their husbands. That is the one thing the modern woman never understands.

LADY MARKBY. And a very good thing too, dear, I dare say. It might break up many a happy home if they did. Not yours, I need hardly say, Gertrude. You have married a pattern husband. I wish I could say as much for myself. But since Sir John has taken to attending the debates regularly, which he never used to do in the good old days, his language has become quite impossible. He always seems to think that he is addressing the House, and consequently whenever he discusses the state of the agricultural labourer, or the Welsh Church, or something quite improper of that kind, I am obliged to send all the servants out of the room. It is not pleasant to see one's own butler, who has been with one for twenty-three years, actually blushing at the side-board, and the footmen making contortions in corners like persons in circuses. I assure you my life will be quite ruined unless they send John at once to the Upper House. He won't take any interest in politics then, will he? The House of Lords is so sensible. An assembly of gentlemen. But in his present state, Sir John is really a great trial. Why, this morning before breakfast was half-over, he stood up on the hearth-rug, put his hands in his pockets, and appealed to the country at the top of his voice. I left the table as soon as I had my second cup of tea, I need hardly say. But his violent language could be heard all over the house! I trust, Gertrude, that Sir Robert is not like that?

LADY CHILTERN. But I am very much interested in politics, Lady Markby. I love to hear Robert talk about them.

LADY MARKBY. Well, I hope he is not as devoted to Blue Books as Sir John is. I don't think they can be quite improving reading for anyone.

MRS CHEVELEY (*languidly*). I have never read a Blue Book. I prefer books . . . in yellow covers.

LADY MARKBY (*genially unconscious*). Yellow is a gayer colour, is it not? I used to wear yellow a good deal in my early days, and would do so now if Sir John was not so painfully personal in his observations, and a man on the question of dress is always ridiculous, is he not?

MRS CHEVELEY. Oh, no! I think men are the only authorities on dress.

LADY MARKBY. Really? One wouldn't say so from the sort of hats they wear, would one?

The butler enters, followed by the footman. Tea is set on a small table close to LADY CHILTERN.

LADY CHILTERN. May I give you some tea, Mrs Cheveley?

MRS CHEVELEY. Thanks.

The butler hands MRS CHEVELEY *a cup of tea on a salver.*

LADY CHILTERN. Some tea, Lady Markby?

LADY MARKBY. No thanks, dear. (*The servants go out.*) The fact is, I have promised to go round for ten minutes to see poor Lady Brancaster, who is in very great trouble. Her daughter, quite a well-brought-up girl, too, has actually become engaged to be married to a curate in Shropshire. It is very sad, very sad indeed. I can't understand this modern mania for curates. In my time we girls saw them, of course, running about the place like rabbits. But we never took any notice of them, I need hardly say. But I am told that nowadays country society is quite honeycombed with them. I think it most irreligious. And then the eldest son has quarrelled with his father, and it is said that when they meet at the club Lord Brancaster always hides himself behind the money article in *The Times*. However, I believe that is quite a common occurrence nowadays and that they have to take in extra copies of *The Times* at all the clubs in St James's Street; there are so many sons who won't have anything to do with their fathers, and so many fathers who won't speak to their sons. I think myself, it is very much to be regretted.

MRS CHEVELEY. So do I. Fathers have so much to learn from their sons nowadays.

LADY MARKBY. Really, dear? What?

MRS CHEVELEY. The art of living. The only really Fine Art we have produced in modern times.

LADY MARKBY (*shaking her head*). Ah! I am afraid Lord Brancaster knew a good deal about that. More than his poor wife ever did. (*Turning to* LADY CHILTERN.) You know Lady Brancaster, don't you, dear?

LADY CHILTERN. Just slightly. She was staying at Langton last autumn, when we were there.

LADY MARKBY. Well, like all stout women, she looks the very picture of happiness, as no doubt you noticed. But there are many tragedies in her family, besides this affair of the curate. Her own sister, Mrs Jekyll, had a most unhappy life; through no fault of her own, I am sorry to say. She ultimately was so broken-hearted that she went into a convent, or on to the operatic stage, I forget which. No; I think it was decorative art-needlework she took up. I know she had lost all sense of pleasure in life. (*Rising.*) And now, Gertrude, if you will allow me, I shall leave Mrs Cheveley in your charge and call back for her in a quarter of an hour.

Or perhaps, dear Mrs Cheveley, you wouldn't mind waiting in the carriage while I am with Lady Brancaster. As I intend it to be a visit of condolence, I shan't stay long.

MRS CHEVELEY (*rising*). I don't mind waiting in the carriage at all, provided there is somebody to look at one.

LADY MARKBY. Well, I hear the curate is always prowling about the house.

MRS CHEVELEY. I am afraid I am not fond of girl friends.

LADY CHILTERN (*rising*). Oh, I hope Mrs Cheveley will stay here a little. I should like to have a few minute's conversation with her.

MRS CHEVELEY. How very kind of you, Lady Chiltern! Believe me, nothing would give me greater pleasure.

LADY MARKBY. Ah! no doubt you both have many pleasant reminiscences of your schooldays to talk over together. Good-bye, dear Gertrude! Shall I see you at Lady Bonar's tonight? She has discovered a wonderful new genius. He does . . . nothing at all, I believe. That is a great comfort, is it not?

LADY CHILTERN. Robert and I are dining at home by ourselves tonight, and I don't think I shall go anywhere afterwards. Robert, of course, will have to be in the House. But there is nothing interesting on.

LADY MARKBY. Dining at home by yourselves? Is that quite prudent? Ah, I forgot, your husband is an exception. Mine is the general rule, and nothing ages a woman so rapidly as having married the general rule.

Exit LADY MARKBY.

MRS CHEVELEY. Wonderful woman, Lady Markby, isn't she? Talks more and says less than anybody I ever met. She is made to be a public speaker. Much more so than her husband, though he is a typical Englishman, always dull and usually violent.

LADY CHILTERN (*makes no answer, but remains standing. There is a pause. Then the eyes of the two women meet.* LADY CHILTERN *looks stern and pale.* MRS CHEVELEY *seems rather amused*). Mrs Cheveley, I think it is right to tell you quite frankly that, had I known who you really were, I should not have invited you to my house last night.

MRS CHEVELEY (*with an impertinent smile*). Really?

LADY CHILTERN. I could not have done so.

MRS CHEVELEY. I see that after all these years you have not changed a bit, Gertrude.

LADY CHILTERN. I never change.

MRS CHEVELEY (*elevating her eyebrows*). Then life has taught you nothing?

LADY CHILTERN. It has taught me that a person who has once been guilty of a dishonest and dishonourable action may be guilty of it a second time, and should be shunned.

MRS CHEVELEY. Would you apply that rule to everyone?

LADY CHILTERN. Yes, to everyone, without exception.

MRS CHEVELEY. Then I am sorry for you, Gertrude, very sorry for you.

LADY CHILTERN. You see now, I am sure, that for many reasons any further acquaintance between us during your stay in London is quite impossible?

MRS CHEVELEY (*leaning back, in her chair*). Do you know, Gertrude, I don't mind your talking morality a bit. Morality is simply the attitude we adopt towards people whom we personally dislike. You dislike me. I am quite aware of that. And I have always detested you. And yet I have come here to do you a service.

LADY CHILTERN (*contemptuously*). Like the service you wished to render my husband last night, I suppose. Thank heaven, I saved him from that.

MRS CHEVELEY (*starting to her feet*). It was you who made him write that insolent letter to me? It was you who made him break his promise?

LADY CHILTERN. Yes.

MRS CHEVELEY. Then you must make him keep it. I give you till tomorrow morning – no more. If by that time your husband does not solemnly bind himself to help me in this great scheme in which I am interested –

LADY CHILTERN. This fraudulent speculation –

MRS CHEVELEY. Call it what you choose. I hold your husband in the hollow of my hand, and if you are wise you will make him do what I tell him.

LADY CHILTERN (*rising and going towards her*). You are impertinent. What has my husband to do with you? With a woman like you?

MRS CHEVELEY (*with a bitter laugh*). In this world like meets like. It is because your husband is himself fraudulent and dishonest that we pair so well together. Between you and him there are chasms. He and I are closer than friends. We are enemies linked together. The same sin binds us.

LADY CHILTERN. How dare you class my husband with yourself? How dare you threaten him or me? Leave my house. You are unfit to enter it.

SIR ROBERT CHILTERN *enters from behind. He hears his wife's last words, and sees to whom they are addressed. He grows deadly pale.*

MRS CHEVELEY. Your house! A house bought with the price of dishonour. A house, everything in which has been paid for by fraud. (*Turns round and sees* SIR ROBERT CHILTERN.) Ask him what the origin of his fortune is! Get him to tell you how he sold to a stockbroker a Cabinet secret. Learn from him to what you owe your position.

LADY CHILTERN. It is not true! Robert! It is not true!

MRS CHEVELEY (*pointing at him with outstretched finger*). Look at him! Can he deny it? Does he dare to?

SIR ROBERT CHILTERN. Go! Go at once. You have done your worst now.

MRS CHEVELEY. My worst? I have not yet finished with you, with either of you. I give you both till tomorrow at noon. If by then you don't do what I bid you to do, the whole world shall know the origin of Robert Chiltern.

SIR ROBERT CHILTERN *strikes the bell. Enter* MASON.

SIR ROBERT CHILTERN. Show Mrs Cheveley out.

MRS CHEVELEY *starts; then bows with somewhat exaggerated politeness to* LADY CHILTERN, *who makes no sign of response. As she passes by* SIR ROBERT CHILTERN, *who is standing close to the door, she pauses for a moment and looks him straight in the face. She then goes out, followed by the servant, who closes the door after him. The husband and wife are left alone.* LADY CHILTERN *stands like someone in a dreadful dream. Then she turns round and looks at her husband. She looks at him with strange eyes, as though she was seeing him for the first time.*

LADY CHILTERN. You sold a Cabinet secret for money! You began your life with fraud! You built up your career on dishonour! Oh, tell me it is not true! Lie to me! Lie to me! Tell me it is not true!

SIR ROBERT CHILTERN. What this woman said is quite true. But, Gertrude, listen to me. You don't realise how I was tempted. Let me tell you the whole thing.

Goes towards her.

LADY CHILTERN. Don't come near me. Don't touch me. I feel as if you had soiled me for ever. Oh! what a mask you have been wearing all these years! A horrible painted mask! You sold your self for money. Oh! a common thief were better. You put yourself up to sale to the highest bidder! You were bought in the market. You lie to the whole world. And yet you will not lie to me.

SIR ROBERT CHILTERN (*rushing towards her*). Gertrude! Gertrude!

LADY CHILTERN (*thrusting him back with outstretched hands*). No, don't speak! Say nothing! Your voice wakes terrible memories – memories of things that made me love you – memories of words that made me love you – memories that now are horrible to me. And how I worshipped you! You were to me something apart from common life, a thing pure, noble, honest, without stain. The world seemed to me finer because you were in it, and goodness more real because you lived. And now – oh, when I think that I made of a man like you my ideal! the ideal of my life!

SIR ROBERT CHILTERN. There was your mistake. There was your error. The error all women commit. Why can't you women love us, faults and all? Why do you place us on monstrous pedestals? We have all feet of clay, women as well as men: but when we men love women, we love them knowing their weaknesses, their follies, their imperfections, love them all the more, it may be, for that reason. It is not the perfect, but the imperfect, who have need of love. It is when we are wounded by our own hands, or by the hands of others, that love should come to cure us – else what use is love at all? All sins, except a sin against itself, Love should forgive. All lives, save loveless lives, true Love should pardon. A man's love is like that. It is wider, larger, more human than a woman's. Women think that they are making ideals of men. What they are making of us are false idols merely. You made your false idol of me, and I had not the courage to come down, show you my wounds, tell you my weaknesses. I was afraid that I might lose your love, as I have lost it now. And so, last night you ruined my life for me – yes, ruined it! What this woman asked of me was nothing compared to what she offered to me. She offered security, peace, stability. The sin of my youth, that I had thought was buried, rose up in front of me, hideous, horrible, with its hands at my throat. I could have killed it for ever, sent it back into its tomb, destroyed its record, burned the one witness against me. You prevented me. No one but you, you know it. And now what is there before me but public disgrace, ruin, terrible shame, the mockery of the world, a lonely dishonoured life, a lonely dishonoured death, it may be, some day? Let women make no more ideals of men! let them not put them on altars and bow before them, or they may ruin other lives as completely as you – you whom I have so wildly loved – have ruined mine!

He passes from the room. LADY CHILTERN *rushes towards him, but the door is closed when she reaches it. Pale with anguish, bewildered, helpless, she sways like a plant in the water. Her hands, outstretched, seem to tremble in the air like blossoms in the wind. Then she flings herself down beside a sofa and buries her face. Her sobs are like the sobs of a child.*

Act drop.

THIRD ACT

Scene: the Library in Lord Goring's house. An Adam room. On the right is the door leading into the hall. On the left, the door of the smoking-room. A pair of folding doors at the back open into the drawing-room. The fire is lit. Phipps, the Butler, is arranging some newspapers on the writing-table. The distinction of Phipps is his impassivity. He has been termed by enthusiasts the Ideal Butler. The Sphinx is not so incommunicable. He is a mask with a manner. Of his intellectual or emotional life, history knows nothing. He represents the dominance of form.

Enter LORD GORING *in evening dress with a buttonhole. He is wearing a silk hat and Inverness cape. White-gloved, he carries a Louis Seize cane. His are all the delicate fopperies of Fashion. One sees that he stands in immediate relation to modern life, makes it indeed, and so masters it. He is the first well-dressed philosopher in the history of thought.*

LORD GORING. Got my second buttonhole for me, Phipps?

PHIPPS: Yes, my lord.

Takes his hat, cane, and cape, and presents new buttonhole on salver.

LORD GORING. Rather distinguished thing, Phipps. I am the only person of the smallest importance in London at present who wears a buttonhole.

PHIPPS. Yes, my lord. I have observed that.

LORD GORING (*taking out old buttonhole*). You see, Phipps, Fashion is what one wears oneself. What is unfashionable is what other people wear.

PHIPPS. Yes, my lord.

LORD GORING. Just as vulgarity is simply the conduct of other people.

PHIPPS. Yes, my lord.

LORD GORING (*putting in new buttonhole*). And falsehoods the truths of other people.

PHIPPS. Yes, my lord.

LORD GORING. Other people are quite dreadful. The only possible society is oneself,

PHIPPS. Yes, my lord.

LORD GORING. To love oneself is the beginning of a lifelong romance, Phipps.

PHIPPS. Yes, my lord.

LORD GORING (*looking at himself in the glass*). Don't think I quite like this buttonhole, Phipps. Makes me look a little too old. Makes me almost in the prime of life, eh, Phipps?

PHIPPS. I don't observe any alteration in your lordship's appearance.

LORD GORING. You don't, Phipps?

PHIPPS. No, my lord.

LORD GORING. I am not quite sure. For the future a more trivial buttonhole, Phipps, on Thursday evenings.

PHIPPS. I will speak to the florist, my lord. She has had a loss in her family lately, which perhaps accounts for the lack of triviality your lordship complains of in the buttonhole.

LORD GORING. Extraordinary thing about the lower class in England – they are always losing their relations.

PHIPPS. Yes, my lord! They are extremely fortunate in that respect.

LORD GORING (*turns round and looks at him.* PHIPPS *remains impassive*). Hum! Any letters, Phipps?

PHIPPS. Three, my lord. (*Hands letters on a salver.*)

LORD GORING (*takes letters*). Want my cab round in twenty minutes.

PHIPPS. Yes, my lord.

Goes towards door.

LORD GORING (*holds up letter in pink envelope*). Ahem! Phipps, when did this letter arrive?

PHIPPS. It was brought by hand just after your lordship went to the club.

LORD GORING. That will do. (*Exit PHIPPS.*) Lady Chiltern's handwriting on Lady Chiltern's pink notepaper. That is rather curious. I thought Robert was to write. Wonder what Lady Chiltern has got to say to me? (*Sits at bureau, opens letter, and reads it.*) 'I want you. I trust you. I am coming to you. Gertrude.' (*Puts down the letter with a puzzled look. Then takes it up, and reads it again slowly.*) 'I want you. I trust you. I am coming to you.' So she has found out everything! Poor woman! Poor woman! (*Pulls out watch and looks at it.*) But what an hour to call! Ten o'clock! I shall have to give up going to the Berkshires'. However, it is always nice to be expected, and not to arrive. I am not expected at the Bachelors', so I shall certainly go there. Well, I will make her stand by her husband. That is the only thing for her to do. That is the only thing for any woman to do. It is the growth of the moral sense in women that makes marriage such a hopeless, one-sided institution. Ten o'clock. She should be here soon. I must tell Phipps I am not in to anyone else.

Goes towards bell.

Enter PHIPPS.

PHIPPS. Lord Caversham.

LORD GORING. Oh, why will parents always appear at the wrong time? Some extraordinary mistake in nature, I suppose. (*Enter LORD CAVERSHAM.*) Delighted to see you, my dear father.

Goes to meet him.

LORD CAVERSHAM. Take my cloak off.

LORD GORING. Is it worth while, father?

LORD CAVERSHAM. Of course it is worth while, sir. Which is the most comfortable chair?

LORD GORING. This one, father. It is the chair I use myself, when I have visitors.

LORD CAVERSHAM. Thank ye. No draught, I hope, in this room?

LORD GORING. No, father.

LORD CAVERSHAM (*sitting down*). Glad to hear it. Can't stand draughts. No draughts at home.

LORD GORING. Good many breezes, father.

LORD CAVERSHAM. Eh? Eh? Don't understand what you mean. Want to have a serious conversation with you, sir.

LORD GORING. My dear father! At this hour?

LORD CAVERSHAM. Well, sir, it is only ten o'clock. What is your objection to the hour? I think the hour is an admirable hour!

LORD GORING Well, the fact is, father, this is not my day for talking seriously. I am very sorry, but it is not my day.

LORD CAVERSHAM. What do you mean, sir?.

LORD GORING. During the Season, father, I only talk seriously on the first Tuesday in every month, from four to seven.

LORD CAVERSHAM. Well, make it Tuesday, sir, make it Tuesday.

LORD GORING. But it is after seven, father, and my doctor says I must not have any serious conversation after seven. It makes me talk in my sleep.

LORD CAVERSHAM. Talk in your sleep, sir? What does that matter? You are not married.

LORD GORING. No, father, I am not married.

LORD CAVERSHAM. Hum! That is what I have come to talk to you about, sir. You have got to get married, and at once. Why, when I was your age, sir, I had been an inconsolable widower for three months, and was already paying my addresses to your admirable mother. Damme, sir, it is your duty to get married. You can't be always living for pleasure. Every man of position is married nowadays. Bachelors are not fashionable any more. They are a damaged lot. Too much is known about them. You must get a wife, sir. Look where your friend Robert Chiltern has got to by probity, hard work, and a sensible marriage with a good woman. Why don't you imitate him, sir? Why don't you take him for your model?

LORD GORING. I think I shall, father.

LORD CAVERSHAM. I wish you would, sir. Then I should be happy. At present I make your mother's life miserable on your account. You are heartless, sir, quite heartless.

LORD GORING I hope not, father.

LORD CAVERSHAM. And it is high time for you to get married. You are thirty-four years of age, sir.

LORD GORING. Yes, father, but I only admit to thirty-two – thirty-one and half when I have a really good buttonhole. This buttonhole is not . . . trivial enough.

LORD CAVERSHAM. I tell you you are thirty-four, sir. And there is a draught in your room, besides, which makes your conduct worse. Why did you tell me there was no draught, sir? I feel a draught, sir, I feel it distinctly.

LORD GORING. So do I, father. It is a dreadful draught. I will come and see you tomorrow, father. We can talk over anything you like. Let me help you on with your cloak, father.

LORD CAVERSHAM. No, sir; I have called this evening for a definite purpose, and I am going to see it through at all costs to my health or yours. Put down my cloak, sir.

LORD GORING. Certainly, father. But let us go into another room. (*Rings bell.*) There is a dreadful draught here. (*Enter* PHIPPS.) Phipps, is there a good fire in the smoking-room?

PHIPPS. Yes, my lord.

LORD GORING. Come in there, father. Your sneezes are quite heart-rending.

LORD CAVERSHAM. Well, sir, I suppose I have a right to sneeze when I choose?

LORD GORING (*apologetically*). Quite so, father. I was merely expressing sympathy.

LORD CAVERSHAM. Oh, damn sympathy. There is a great deal too much of that sort of thing going on nowadays.

LORD GORING. I quite agree with you, father. If there was less sympathy in the world there would be less trouble in the world.

LORD CAVERSHAM (*going towards the smoking-room*). That is a paradox, sir. I hate paradoxes.

LORD GORING. So do I, father. Everybody one meets is a paradox nowadays. It is a great bore. It makes society so obvious.

LORD CAVERSHAM (*turning round, and looking at his son beneath his bushy eyebrows*). Do you always really understand what you say, sir?

LORD GORING (*after some hesitation*). Yes, father, if I listen attentively.

LORD CAVERSHAM (*indignantly*). If you listen attentively! . . . Conceited young puppy!

Goes off grumbling into the smoking-room. PHIPPS *enters.*

LORD GORING. Phipps, there is a lady coming to see me this evening on particular business. Show her into the drawing-room when she arrives. You understand?

PHIPPS. Yes, my lord.

LORD GORING It is a matter of the gravest importance, Phipps.

PHIPPS. I understand, my lord.

LORD GORING. No one else is to be admitted, under any circumstances.

PHIPPS. I understand, my lord.

Bell rings.

LORD GORING. Ah! that is probably the lady. I shall see her myself.

Just as he is going towards the door LORD CAVERSHAM *enters from the smoking-room.*

LORD CAVERSHAM. Well, sir? am I to wait attendance on you?

LORD GORING (*considerably perplexed*). In a moment, father.
Do excuse me. (LORD CAVERSHAM *goes back*.) Well,
remember my instructions, Phipps – into that room.

PHIPPS. Yes, my lord.

LORD GORING *goes into the smoking-room.* HAROLD, *the
footman, shows* MRS CHEVELEY *in. Lamia-like, she is in green
and silver. She has a cloak of black satin, lined with dead rose-leaf
silk.*

HAROLD. What name, madam?

MRS CHEVELEY (*to* PHIPPS, *who advances towards her*). Is
Lord Goring not here? I was told he was at home?

PHIPPS. His lordship is engaged at present with Lord
Caversham, madam.

Turns a cold, glassy eye on HAROLD, *who at once retires.*

MRS CHEVELEY (*to herself*). How very filial!

PHIPPS. His lordship told me to ask you, madam, to be kind
enough to wait in the drawing-room for him. His lordship
will come to you there.

MRS CHEVELEY (*with a look of surprise*). Lord Goring expects
me?

PHIPPS. Yes, madam.

MRS CHEVELEY. Are you quite sure?

PHIPPS. His lordship told me that if a lady called I was to ask
her to wait in the drawing-room. (*Goes to the door of the
drawing-room and opens it*.) His lordship's directions on the
subject were very precise.

MRS CHEVELEY (*to herself*). How thoughtful of him! To expect
the unexpected shows a thoroughly modern intellect. (*Goes
towards the drawing-room and looks in*.) Ugh! How dreary a
bachelor's drawing-room always looks. I shall have to alter
all this. (PHIPPS *brings the lamp from the writing-table*.) No,
I don't care for that lamp. It is far too glaring. Light some
candles.

PHIPPS (*replaces lamp*). Certainly, madam.

MRS CHEVELEY. I hope the candles have very becoming shades.

PHIPPS. We have had no complaints about them, madam, as yet.

Passes into the drawing-room and begins to light the candles.

MRS CHEVELEY (*to herself*). I wonder what woman he is waiting for tonight. It will be delightful to catch him. Men always look so silly when they are caught. And they are always being caught. (*Looks about room and approaches the writing-table.*) What a very interesting room! What a very interesting picture! Wonder what his correspondence is like. (*Takes up letters.*) Oh, what a very uninteresting correspondence! Bills and cards, debts and dowagers! Who on earth writes to him on pink paper? How silly to write on pink paper! It looks like the beginning of a middle-class romance. Romance should never begin with sentiment. It should begin with science and end with a settlement. (*Puts letter down, then takes it up again.*) I know that handwriting. That is Gertrude Chiltern's. I remember it perfectly. The ten commandments in every stroke of the pen, and the moral law all over the page. Wonder what Gertrude is writing to him about? Something horrid about me, I suppose. How I detest that woman! (*Reads it.*) 'I trust you. I want you. I am coming to you. Gertrude!' 'I trust you. I want you. I am coming to you.'

A look of triumph comes over her face. She is just about to steal the letter, when PHIPPS *comes in.*

PHIPPS. The candles in the drawing-room are lit, madam, as you directed.

MRS CHEVELEY. Thank you.

Rises hastily and slips the letter under a large silver-cased blotting-book that is lying on the table.

PHIPPS. I trust the shades will be to your liking, madam. They are the most becoming we have. They are the same as his lordship uses himself when he is dressing for dinner.

MRS CHEVELEY (*with a smile*). Then I am sure they will he perfectly right.

PHIPPS (*gravely*). Thank you, madam

MRS CHEVELEY *goes into the drawing-room.* PHIPPS *closes the door and retires. The door is then slowly opened, and* MRS CHEVELEY *comes out and creeps stealthily towards the writing-table. Suddenly voices are heard from the smoking-room.* MRS CHEVELEY *grows pale, and stops. The voices grow louder, and she goes back into the drawing-room, biting her lip.*

Enter LORD GORING *and* LORD CAVERSHAM.

LORD GORING (*expostulating*). My dear father, if I am to get married, surely you will allow me to choose the time, place, and person? Particularly the person.

LORD CAVERSHAM (*testily*). That is a matter for me, sir. You would probably make a very poor choice. It is I who should be consulted, not you. There is property at stake. It is not a matter for affection. Affection comes later on in married life.

LORD GORING. Yes. In married life affection comes when people thoroughly dislike each other, father, doesn't it?

Puts on LORD CAVERSHAM's *cloak for him.*

LORD CAVERSHAM. Certainly, sir. I mean certainly not, sir. You are talking very foolishly tonight. What I say is that marriage is a matter for common sense.

LORD GORING. But women who have common sense are so curiously plain, father, aren't they? Of course I only speak from hearsay.

LORD CAVERSHAM. No woman, plain or pretty, has any common sense at all, sir. Common sense is the privilege of our sex.

LORD GORING. Quite so. And we men are so self-sacrificing that we never use it, do we, father?

LORD CAVERSHAM. I use it, sir. I use nothing else.

LORD GORING. So my mother tells me.

LORD CAVERSHAM. It is the secret of your mother's happiness. You are very heartless, sir, very heartless.

LORD GORING. I hope not, father.

Goes out for a moment. Then returns, looking rather put out, with SIR ROBERT CHILTERN.

SIR ROBERT CHILTERN. My dear Arthur, what a piece of good luck meeting you on the doorstep! Your servant had just told me you were not at home. How extraordinary!

LORD GORING. The fact is, I am horribly busy tonight, Robert, and I gave orders I was not at home to anyone. Even my father had a comparatively cold reception. He complained of a draught the whole time.

SIR ROBERT CHILTERN. Ah! you must be at home to me, Arthur. You are my best friend. Perhaps by tomorrow you will be my only friend. My wife has discovered everything.

LORD GORING. Ah! I guessed as much!

SIR ROBERT CHILTERN (*looking at him*). Really! How?

LORD GORING (*after some hesitation*). Oh merely by something in the expression of your face as you came in. Who told her?

SIR ROBERT CHILTERN. Mrs Cheveley herself. And the woman I love knows that I began my career with an act of low dishonesty, that I built up my life upon sands of shame – that I sold, like a common huckster, the secret that had been entrusted to me as a man of honour. I thank heaven poor Lord Radley died without knowing that I betrayed him. I would to God I had died before I had been so horribly tempted, or had fallen so low.

Burying his face in his hands.

LORD GORING (*after a pause*). You have heard nothing from Vienna yet, in answer to your wire?

SIR ROBERT CHILTERN (*looking up*). Yes; I got a telegram from the first secretary at eight o'clock tonight.

LORD GORING. Well?

SIR ROBERT CHILTERN. Nothing is absolutely known against her. On the contrary, she occupies a rather high position in society. It is a sort of open secret that Baron

Arnheim left her the greater portion of his immense fortune. Beyond that I can learn nothing.

LORD GORING. She doesn't turn out to be a spy, then?

SIR ROBERT CHILTERN. Oh! spies are of no use nowadays. Their profession is over. The newspapers do their work instead.

LORD GORING. And thunderingly well they do it.

SIR ROBERT CHILTERN. Arthur, I am parched with thirst. May I ring for something? Some hock and seltzer?

LORD GORING. Certainly. Let me.

Rings the bell.

SIR ROBERT CHILTERN. Thanks! I don't know what to do. Arthur, I don't know what to do, and you are my only friend. But what a friend you are – the one friend I can trust. I can trust you absolutely, can't I?

Enter PHIPPS.

LORD GORING. My dear Robert, of course. Oh! (*To* PHIPPS.) Bring some hock and seltzer.

PHIPPS. Yes, my lord.

LORD GORING. And Phipps!

PHIPPS. Yes, my lord.

LORD GORING. Will you excuse me for a moment, Robert? I want to give some directions to my servant.

SIR ROBERT CHILTERN. Certainly.

LORD GORING. When that lady calls, tell her that I am not expected home this evening. Tell her that I have been suddenly called out of town. You understand?

PHIPPS. The lady is in that room, my lord. You told me to show her into that room, my lord.

LORD GORING. You did perfectly right. (*Exit* PHIPPS.) What a mess I am in. No; I think I shall get through it. I'll give her a lecture through the door. Awkward thing to manage, though.

SIR ROBERT CHILTERN. Arthur, tell me what I should do. My life seems to have crumbled about me, I am a ship without a rudder in a night without a star.

LORD GORING. Robert, you love your wife, don't you?

SIR ROBERT CHILTERN. I love her more than anything in the world. I used to think ambition the great thing. It is not. Love is the great thing in the world. There is nothing but love, and I love her. But I am defamed in her eyes. I am ignoble in her eyes. There is a wide gulf between us now. She has found me out, Arthur, she has found me out.

LORD GORING. Has she never in her life done some folly – some indiscretion – that she should not forgive your sin?

SIR ROBERT CHILTERN. My wife! Never! She does not know what weakness or temptation is. I am of clay like other men. She stands apart as good women do – pitiless in her perfection – cold and stern and without mercy. But I love her, Arthur. We are childless, and I have no one else to love, no one else to love me. Perhaps if God had sent us children she might have been kinder to me. But God has given us a lonely house. And she has cut my heart in two. Don't let us talk of it. I was brutal to her this evening. But I suppose when sinners talk to saints they are brutal always. I said to her things that were hideously true, on my side, from my standpoint, from the standpoint of men. But don't let us talk of that.

LORD GORING. Your wife will forgive you. Perhaps at this moment she is forgiving you. She loves you, Robert. Why should she not forgive?

SIR ROBERT CHILTERN. God grant it! God grant it! (*Buries his face in his hands.*) But there is something more I have to tell you, Arthur.

Enter PHIPPS *with drinks.*

PHIPPS (*hands hock and selzer to* SIR ROBERT CHILTERN). Hock and seltzer, sir.

SIR ROBERT CHILTERN. Thank you.

LORD GORING. Is your carriage here, Robert?

SIR ROBERT CHILTERN. No; I walked from the club.

LORD GORING. Sir Robert will take my cab, Phipps.

PHIPPS. Yes, my lord.

Exit.

LORD GORING. Robert, you don't mind my sending you away?

SIR ROBERT CHILTERN. Arthur, you must let me stay for five minutes. I have made up my mind what I am going to do tonight in the House. The debate on the Argentine Canal is to begin at eleven. (*A chair falls in the drawing-room.*) What is that?

LORD GORING. Nothing.

SIR ROBERT CHILTERN. I heard a chair fall in the next room. Someone has been listening.

LORD GORING. No, no; there is no one there.

SIR ROBERT CHILTERN. There is someone. There are lights in the room, and the door is ajar. Someone has been listening to every secret of my life. Arthur, what does this mean?

LORD GORING. Robert, you are excited, unnerved. I tell you there is no one in that room. Sit down, Robert.

SIR ROBERT CHILTERN. Do you give me your word that there is no one there?

LORD GORING. Yes.

SIR ROBERT CHILTERN. Your word of honour?

Sits down.

LORD GORING. Yes.

SIR ROBERT CHILTERN (*rises*). Arthur, let me see for myself.

LORD GORING. No, no.

SIR ROBERT CHILTERN. If there is no one there why should I not look in that room? Arthur, you must let me go into that room and satisfy myself. Let me know that no eaves-dropper has heard my life's secret. Arthur, you don't realise what I am going through.

LORD GORING. Robert, this must stop. I have told you that there is no one in that room – that is enough.

SIR ROBERT CHILTERN (*rushes to the door of the room*). It is not enough. I insist on going into this room. You have told me there is no one there, so what reason can you have for refusing me?

LORD GORING. For God's sake, don't! There is someone there. Someone whom you must not see.

SIR ROBERT CHILTERN. Ah, I thought so!

LORD GORING. I forbid you to enter that room.

SIR ROBERT CHILTERN. Stand back. My life is at stake. And I don't care who is there. I will know who it is to whom I have told my secret and my shame.

Enters room.

LORD GORING. Great heavens! his own wife!

SIR ROBERT CHILTERN *comes back, with a look of scorn and anger on his face.*

SIR ROBERT CHILTERN. What explanation have you to give me for the presence of that woman here?

LORD GORING. Robert, I swear to you on my honour that that lady is stainless and guiltless of all offence towards you.

SIR ROBERT CHILTERN. She is a vile, an infamous thing!

LORD GORING. Don't say that, Robert! It was for your sake she came here. It was to try and save you she came here. She loves you and no one else.

SIR ROBERT CHILTERN. You are mad. What have I to do with her intrigues with you? Let her remain your mistress! You are well suited to each other. She, corrupt and shameful – you, false as a friend, treacherous as an enemy even –

LORD GORING. It is not true, Robert. Before heaven, it is not true. In her presence and in yours I will explain all.

SIR ROBERT CHILTERN. Let me pass, sir. You have lied enough upon your word of honour.

SIR ROBERT CHILTERN *goes out.* LORD GORING *rushes to the door of the drawing-room, when* MRS CHEVELEY *comes out, looking radiant and much amused.*

MRS CHEVELEY (*with a mock curtsey*). Good evening, Lord Goring!

LORD GORING. Mrs Cheveley! Great heavens! . . . May I ask what you were doing in my drawing-room?

MRS CHEVELEY. Merely listening. I have a perfect passion for listening through keyholes. One always hears such wonderful things through them.

LORD GORING. Doesn't that sound rather like tempting Providence?

MRS CHEVELEY. Oh! surely Providence can resist temptation by this time.

Makes a sign to him to take her cloak off, which he does.

LORD GORING. I am glad you have called. I am going to give you some good advice.

MRS CHEVELEY. Oh! pray don't. One should never give a woman anything that she can't wear in the evening.

LORD GORING. I see you are quite as wilful as you used to be.

MRS CHEVELEY. Far more! I have greatly improved. I have had more experience.

LORD GORING. Too much experience is a dangerous thing. Pray have a cigarette. Half the pretty women in London smoke cigarettes. Personally I prefer the other half.

MRS CHEVELEY. Thanks. I never smoke. My dressmaker wouldn't like it, and a woman's first duty in life is to her dressmaker, isn't it? What the second duty is, no one has as yet discovered.

LORD GORING. You have come here to sell me Robert Chiltern's letter, haven't you?

MRS CHEVELEY. To offer it to you on conditions. How did you guess that?

LORD GORING. Because you haven't mentioned the subject. Have you got it with you?

MRS CHEVELEY (*sitting down*). Oh, no! A well-made dress has no pockets.

LORD GORING. What is your price for it?

MRS CHEVELEY, How absurdly English you are! The English think that a cheque-book can solve every problem in life. Why, my dear Arthur, I have very much more money than you have, and quite as much as Robert Chiltern has got hold of. Money is not what I want.

LORD GORING. What do you want then, Mrs Cheveley?

MRS CHEVELEY. Why don't you call me Laura?

LORD GORING. I don't like the name.

MRS CHEVELEY. You used to adore it.

LORD GORING. Yes: that's why.

MRS CHEVELEY *motions to him to sit down beside her. He smiles, and does so.*

MRS CHEVELEY. Arthur, you loved me once.

LORD GORING. Yes.

MRS CHEVELEY. And you asked me to be your wife.

LORD GORING. That was the natural result of my loving you.

MRS CHEVELEY. And you threw me over because you saw, or said you saw, poor old Lord Mortlake trying to have a violent flirtation with me in the conservatory at Tenby.

LORD GORING. I am under the impression that my lawyer settled that matter with you on certain terms . . . dictated by yourself.

MRS CHEVELEY. At the time I was poor; you were rich.

LORD GORING. Quite so. That is why you pretended to love me.

MRS CHEVELEY (*shrugging her shoulders*). Poor old Lord Mortlake, who had only two topics of conversation, his gout and his wife! I never could quite make out which of the two he was talking about. He used the most horrible language about them both. Well, you were silly, Arthur. Why, Lord Mortlake was never anything more to me than amusement. One of those utterly tedious amusements one only finds at an English country house on an English country Sunday. I don't think anyone at all morally responsible for what he or she does at an English country house.

LORD GORING. Yes. I know lots of people think that.

MRS CHEVELEY. I loved you, Arthur.

LORD GORING. My dear Mrs Cheveley, you have always been far too clever to know anything about love.

MRS CHEVELEY. I did love you. And you loved me. You know you loved me; and love is a very wonderful thing. I suppose that when a man has once loved a woman, he will do anything for her, except continue to love her?

Puts her hand on his.

LORD GORING (*taking his hand away quietly*). Yes: except that.

MRS CHEVELEY (*after a pause*). I am tired of living abroad. I want to come back to London. I want to have a charming house here. I want to have a salon. If one could only teach the English how to talk, and the Irish how to listen, society here would be quite civilised. Besides, I have arrived at the romantic stage. When I saw you last night at the Chilterns', I knew you were the only person I had ever cared for, if I ever have cared for anybody, Arthur. And so, on the morning of the day you marry me, I will give you Robert Chiltern's letter. That is my offer. I will give it to you now, if you promise to marry me.

LORD GORING. Now?

MRS CHEVELEY (*smiling*). Tomorrow.

LORD GORING. Are you really serious?

MRS CHEVELEY. Yes, quite serious.

LORD GORING. I should make you a very bad husband.

MRS CHEVELEY. I don't mind bad husbands. I have had two. They amused me immensely.

LORD GORING. You mean that you amused yourself immensely, don't you?

MRS CHEVELEY. What do you know about my married life?

LORD GORING. Nothing: but I can read it like a book.

MRS CHEVELEY. What book?

LORD GORING (*rising*). The Book of Numbers.

MRS CHEVELEY. Do you think it is quite charming of you to be so rude to a woman in your own house?

LORD GORING. In the case of very fascinating women, sex is a challenge, not a defence.

MRS CHEVELEY. I suppose that is meant for a compliment. My dear Arthur, women are never disarmed by compliments. Men always are. That is the difference between the two sexes.

LORD GORING. Women are never disarmed by anything, as far as I know them.

MRS CHEVELEY (*after a pause*). Then you are going to allow your greatest friend, Robert Chiltern, to be ruined, rather than marry someone who really has considerable attractions left. I thought you would have risen to some great height of self-sacrifice, Arthur. I think you should. And the rest of your life you could spend in contemplating your own perfections.

LORD GORING. Oh! I do that as it is. And self-sacrifice is a thing that should be put down by law. It is so demoralising to the people for whom one sacrifices oneself. They always go to the bad.

MRS CHEVELEY. As if anything could demoralise Robert Chiltern! You seem to forget that I know his real character.

LORD GORING. What you know about him is not his real character. It was an act of folly done in his youth, dishonourable, I admit, shameful, I admit, unworthy of him, I admit, and therefore . . . not his true character.

MRS CHEVELEY. How you men stand up for each other!

LORD GORING. How you women war against each other!

MRS CHEVELEY (*bitterly*). I only war against one woman, against Gertrude Chiltern. I hate her. I hate her now more than ever.

LORD GORING. Because you have brought a real tragedy into her life, I suppose?

MRS CHEVELEY (*with a sneer*). Oh, there is only one real tragedy in a woman's life. The fact that her past is always her lover, and her future invariably her husband.

LORD GORING. Lady Chiltern knows nothing of the kind of life to which you are alluding.

MRS CHEVELEY. A woman whose size in gloves is seven and three-quarters never knows much about anything. You know Gertrude has always worn seven and three-quarters? That is one of the reasons why there was never any moral sympathy between us . . . Well, Arthur, I suppose this romantic inter-view may be regarded as at an end. You admit it was romantic, don't you? For the privilege of being your wife I was ready to surrender a great prize, the climax of my diplomatic career. You decline. Very well. If Sir Robert doesn't uphold my Argentine scheme, I expose him. *Voilà tout.*

LORD GORING. You mustn't do that. It would be vile, horrible, infamous.

MRS CHEVELEY (*shrugging her shoulders*). Oh! don't use big words. They mean so little. It is a commercial transaction. That is all. There is no good mixing sentimentality in it. I offered to sell Robert Chiltern a certain thing. If he won't pay me my price, he will have to pay the world a greater price. There is no more to be said. I must go. Good-bye. Won't you shake hands?

LORD GORING. With you? No. Your transaction with Robert Chiltern may pass as a loathsome commercial transaction of a loathsome commercial age; but you seem to have forgotten that you came here tonight to talk of love, you whose lips desecrated the word love, you to whom the thing is a book closely sealed, went this afternoon to the house of one of the most noble and gentle women in the world to degrade her husband in her eyes, to try and kill her love for him, to put poison in her heart, and bitterness in her life, to break her idol, and, it may be, spoil her soul. That I cannot forgive you. That was horrible. For that there can be no forgiveness.

MRS CHEVELEY. Arthur, you are unjust to me. Believe me, you are quite unjust to me. I didn't go to taunt Gertrude at all. I had no idea of doing anything of the kind when I entered. I called with Lady Markby simply to ask whether an ornament, a jewel, that I lost somewhere last night, had been found at the Chilterns'. If you don't believe me, you can ask Lady Markby. She will tell you it is true. The scene that occurred happened after Lady Markby had left, and was really forced on me by Gertrude's rudeness and sneers. I called, oh! – a little out of malice if you like – but really to ask if a diamond brooch of mine had been found. That was the origin of the whole thing.

LORD GORING. A diamond snake-brooch with a ruby?

MRS CHEVELEY. Yes. How do you know?

LORD GORING. Because it is found. In point of fact, I found it myself, and stupidly forgot to tell the butler anything about it as I was leaving. (*Goes over to the writing-table and pulls out the drawers.*) It is in this drawer. No, that one. This is the brooch, isn't it?

Holds up the brooch.

MRS CHEVELEY. Yes. I am so glad to get it back. It was . . . a present.

LORD GORING. Won't you wear it?

MRS CHEVELEY. Certainly, if you pin it in. (LORD GORING *suddenly clasps it on her arm.*) Why do you put it on as a bracelet? I never knew it could be worn as a bracelet.

LORD GORING. Really?

MRS CHEVELEY (*holding out her handsome arm*). No; but it looks very well on me as a bracelet, doesn't it?

LORD GORING. Yes; much better than when I saw it last.

MRS CHEVELEY. When did you see it last?

LORD GORING (*calmly*). Oh, ten years ago, on Lady Berkshire, from whom you stole it.

MRS CHEVELEY (*starting*). What do you mean?

LORD GORING. I mean that you stole that ornament from my cousin, Mary Berkshire, to whom I gave it when she was married. Suspicion fell on a wretched servant, who was sent away in disgrace. I recognised it last night. I determined to say nothing about it till I had found the thief. I have found the thief now, and I have heard her own confession.

MRS CHEVELEY (*tossing her head*). It is not true.

LORD GORING. You know it is true. Why, thief is written across your face at this moment.

MRS CHEVELEY. I will deny the whole affair from beginning to end. I will say that I have never seen this wretched thing, that it was never in my possession.

MRS CHEVELEY *tries to get the bracelet off her arm, but fails.* LORD GORING *looks on amused. Her thin fingers tear at the jewel to no purpose. A curse breaks from her.*

LORD GORING. The drawback of stealing a thing, Mrs Cheveley, is that one never knows how wonderful the thing that one steals is. You can't get that bracelet off, unless you know where the spring is. And I see you don't know where the spring is. It is rather difficult to find.

MRS CHEVELEY. You brute! You coward!

She tries again to unclasp the bracelet, but fails.

LORD GORING. Oh! don't use big words. They mean so little.

MRS CHEVELEY (*again tears at the bracelet in a paroxysm of rage, with inarticulate sounds. Then stops, and looks at* LORD GORING). What are you going to do?

LORD GORING. I am going to ring for my servant. He is an admirable servant. Always comes in the moment one rings for him. When he comes I will tell him to fetch the police.

MRS CHEVELEY (*trembling*). The police? What for?

LORD GORING. Tomorrow the Berkshires will prosecute you. That is what the police are for.

MRS CHEVELEY (*is now in an agony of physical terror. Her face is distorted. Her mouth awry. A mask has fallen from her. She is, for the moment, dreadful to look at*). Don't do that. I will do anything you want. Anything in the world you want.

LORD GORING. Give me Robert Chiltern's letter.

MRS CHEVELEY. Stop! Stop! Let me have time to think.

LORD GORING. Give me Robert Chiltern's letter.

MRS CHEVELEY. I have not got it with me. I will give it to you tomorrow.

LORD GORING. You know you are lying. Give it to me at once. (MRS CHEVELEY *pulls the letter out, and hands it to him. She is horribly pale.*) This is it?

MRS CHEVELEY (*in a hoarse voice*). Yes.

LORD GORING (*takes the letter, examines it, sighs, and burns it over the lamp*). For so well-dressed a woman, Mrs Cheveley, you have moments of admirable common sense. I congratulate you.

MRS CHEVELEY (*catches sight of* LADY CHILTERN's *letter, the cover of which is just showing from under the blotting-book*). Please get me a glass of water.

LORD GORING. Certainly.

Goes to the corner of the room and pours out a glass of water. While his back is turned MRS CHEVELEY *steals* LADY CHILTERN's *letter. When* LORD GORING *returns with the glass she refuses it with a gesture.*

MRS CHEVELEY. Thank you. Will you help me on with my cloak?

LORD GORING. With pleasure.

Puts her cloak on.

MRS CHEVELEY. Thanks. I am never going to try to harm Robert Chiltern again.

LORD GORING. Fortunately you have not the chance, Mrs Cheveley.

MRS CHEVELEY. Well, even if I had the chance, I wouldn't. On the contrary, I am going to render him a great service.

LORD GORING. I am charmed to hear it. It is a reformation.

MRS CHEVELEY. Yes. I can't bear so upright a gentleman, so honourable an English gentleman, being so shamefully deceived, and so –

LORD GORING. Well?

MRS CHEVELEY. I find that somehow Gertrude Chiltern's dying speech and confession has strayed into my pocket.

LORD GORING. What do you mean?

MRS CHEVELEY (*with a bitter note of triumph in her voice*). I mean that I am going to send Robert Chiltern the love-letter his wife wrote to you tonight.

LORD GORING. Love-letter?

MRS CHEVELEY (*laughing*). 'I want you. I trust you, I am coming to you. Gertrude.'

LORD GORING *rushes to the bureau and takes up the envelope, finds it empty, and turns round.*

LORD GORING. You wretched woman, must you always be thieving? Give me back that letter. I'll take it from you by force. You shall not leave my room till I have got it.

He rushes towards her, but MRS CHEVELEY *at once puts her hand on the electric bell that is on the table. The bell sounds with shrill reverberations, and* PHIPPS *enters.*

MRS CHEVELEY (*after a pause*). Lord Goring merely rang that you should show me out. Good night, Lord Goring!

Goes out followed by PHIPPS. *Her face is illumined with evil triumph. There is joy in her eyes. Youth seems to have come back to her. Her last glance is like a swift arrow.* LORD GORING *bites his lip, and lights a cigarette.*

Act drop.

FOURTH ACT

Scene: same as Act II.

LORD GORING *is standing by the fireplace with his hands in his pockets. He is looking rather bored.*

LORD GORING (*pulls out his watch, inspects it, and rings the bell*). It is a great nuisance. I can't find anyone in this house to talk to. And I am full of interesting information. I feel like the latest edition of something or other.

Enter SERVANT.

JAMES. Sir Robert is still at the Foreign Office, my lord.

LORD GORING. Lady Chiltern not down yet?

JAMES. Her ladyship has not yet left her room. Miss Chiltern has just come in from riding.

LORD GORING (*to himself*). Ah! that is something.

JAMES. Lord Caversham has been waiting some time in the library for Sir Robert. I told him your lordship was here.

LORD GORING. Thank you. Would you kindly tell him I've gone?

JAMES (*bowing*). I shall do so, my lord.

Exit servant.

LORD GORING. Really, I don't want to meet my father three days running. It is a great deal too much excitement for any son. I hope to goodness he won't come up. Fathers should be neither seen nor heard. That is the only proper basis for family life. Mothers are different. Mothers are darlings.

Throws himself down into a chair, picks up a paper and begins to read it.

Enter LORD CAVERSHAM.

LORD CAVERSHAM. Well, sir, what are you doing here? Wasting your time as usual, I suppose?

LORD GORING (*throws down paper and rises*). My dear father, when one pays a visit it is for the purpose of wasting other people's time, not one's own.

LORD CAVERSHAM. Have you been thinking over what I spoke to you about last night?

LORD GORING. I have been thinking about nothing else.

LORD CAVERSHAM. Engaged to be married yet?

LORD GORING (*genially*). Not yet; but I hope to be before lunchtime.

LORD CAVERSHAM (*caustically*). You can have till dinner-time if it would be of any convenience to you.

LORD GORING. Thanks awfully, but I think I'd sooner be engaged before lunch.

LORD CAVERSHAM. Humph! Never know when you are serious or not.

LORD GORING. Neither do I, father.

A pause.

LORD CAVERSHAM. I suppose you have read *The Times* this morning?

LORD GORING (*airily*). *The Times?* Certainly not. I only read *The Morning Post.* All that one should know about modern life is where the Duchesses are; anything else is quite demoralising.

LORD CAVERSHAM. Do you mean to say you have not read *The Times* leading article on Robert Chiltern's career?

LORD GORING. Good heavens! No. What does it say?

LORD CAVERSHAM. What should it say, sir? Everything complimentary, of course. Chiltern's speech last night on this Argentine Canal scheme was one of the finest pieces of oratory ever delivered in the House since Canning.

LORD GORING. Ah! Never heard of Canning. Never wanted to. And did . . . did Chiltern uphold the scheme?

LORD CAVERSHAM. Uphold it, sir? How little you know him! Why, he denounced it roundly, and the whole system of modern political finance. This speech is the turning-point in his career, as *The Times* points out. You should read this article, sir. (*Opens The Times.*) 'Sir Robert Chiltern. . . . most rising of our young statesmen . . . Brilliant orator . . . Unblemished career . . . Well-known integrity of character . . . Represents what is best in English public life . . . Noble contrast to the lax morality so common among foreign politicians.' They will never say that of you, sir.

LORD GORING. I sincerely hope not, father. However, I am delighted at what you tell me about Robert, thoroughly delighted. It shows he has got pluck.

LORD CAVERSHAM. He has got more than pluck, sir, he has got genius.

LORD GORING. Ah! I prefer pluck. It is not so common, nowadays, as genius is.

LORD CAVERSHAM. I wish you would go into Parliament.

LORD GORING. My dear father, only people who look dull ever get into the House of Commons, and only people who are dull ever succeed there.

LORD CAVERSHAM. Why don't you try to do something useful in life ?

LORD GORING. I am far too young.

LORD CAVERSHAM (*testily*). I hate this affectation of youth, sir. It is a great deal too prevalent nowadays.

LORD GORING. Youth isn't an affectation. Youth is an art.

LORD CAVERSHAM. Why don't you propose to that pretty Miss Chiltern?

LORD GORING. I am of a very nervous disposition, especially in the morning.

LORD CAVERSHAM. I don't suppose there is the smallest chance of her accepting you.

LORD GORING. I don't know how the betting stands today.

LORD CAVERSHAM. If she did accept you she would be the prettiest fool in England.

LORD GORING. That is just what I should like to marry. A thoroughly sensible wife would reduce me to a condition of absolute idiocy in less than six months.

LORD CAVERSHAM. You don't deserve her, sir.

LORD GORING. My dear father, if we men married the women we deserved, we should have a very bad time of it.

Enter MABEL CHILTERN.

MABEL CHILTERN. Oh! . . . How do you do, Lord Caversham? I hope Lady Caversham is quite well?

LORD CAVERSHAM. Lady Caversham is as usual, as usual.

LORD GORING. Good morning, Miss Mabel!

MABEL CHILTERN (*taking no notice at all of* LORD GORING, *and addressing herself exclusively to* LORD CAVERSHAM). And Lady Caversham's bonnets . . . are they at all better?

LORD CAVERSHAM. They have had a serious relapse, I am sorry to say.

LORD GORING. Good morning, Miss Mabel!

MABEL CHILTERN (*to* LORD CAVERSHAM). I hope an operation will not be necessary.

LORD CAVERSHAM (*smiling at her pertness*). If it is, we shall have to give Lady Caversham a narcotic. Otherwise she would never consent to have a feather touched.

LORD GORING (*with increased emphasis*). Good morning, Miss Mabel!

MABEL CHILTERN (*turning round with feigned surprise*). Oh, are you here? Of course you understand that after your breaking your appointment I am never going to speak to you again.

LORD GORING. Oh, please don't say such a thing. You are the one person in London I really like to have to listen to me.

MABEL CHILTERN. Lord Goring, I never believe a single word that either you or I say to each other.

LORD CAVERSHAM. You are quite right, my dear, quite right . . . as far as he is concerned, I mean.

MABEL CHILTERN. Do you think you could possibly make your son behave a little better occasionally? Just as a change.

LORD CAVERSHAM. I regret to say, Miss Chiltern, that I have no influence at all over my son. I wish I had. If I had, I know what I would make him do.

MABEL CHILTERN. I am afraid that he has one of those terribly weak natures that are not susceptible to influence.

LORD CAVERSHAM. He is very heartless, very heartless.

LORD GORING. It seems to me that I am a little in the way here.

MABEL CHILTERN. It is very good for you to be in the way, and to know what people say of you behind your back.

LORD GORING. I don't at all like knowing what people say of me behind my back. It makes me far too conceited.

LORD CAVERSHAM. After that, my dear, I really must bid you good morning.

MABEL CHILTERN. Oh! I hope you are not going to leave me all alone with Lord Goring? Especially at such an early hour in the day.

LORD CAVERSHAM. I am afraid I can't take him with me to Downing Street. It is not the Prime Minister's day for seeing the unemployed.

Shakes hands with MABEL CHILTERN, *takes up his hat and stick, and goes out, with a parting glare of indignation at* LORD GORING.

MABEL CHILTERN (*takes up roses and begins to arrange them in a bowl on the table*). People who don't keep their appointments in the Park are horrid.

LORD GORING. Detestable.

MABEL CHILTERN. I am glad you admit it. But I wish you wouldn't look so pleased about it.

LORD GORING. I can't help it. I always look pleased when I am with you.

MABEL CHILTERN (*sadly*). Then I suppose it is my duty to remain with you?

LORD GORING. Of course it is.

MABEL CHILTERN. Well, my duty is a thing I never do, on principle. It always depresses me. So I am afraid I must leave you.

LORD GORING. Please don't, Miss Mabel. I have something very particular to say to you.

MABEL CHILTERN (*rapturously*). Oh, is it a proposal ?

LORD GORING (*somewhat taken aback*). Well, yes, it is – I am bound to say it is.

MABEL CHILTERN (*with a sigh of pleasure*). I am so glad. That makes the second today.

LORD GORING (*indignantly*). The second today? What conceited ass has been impertinent enough to dare to propose to you before I had proposed to you?

MABEL CHILTERN. Tommy Trafford, of course. It is one of Tommy's days for proposing. He always proposes on Tuesdays and Thursdays, during the Season.

LORD GORING. You didn't accept him, I hope?

MABEL CHILTERN. I make it a rule never to accept Tommy. That is why he goes on proposing. Of course, as you didn't turn up this morning, I very nearly said yes. It would have been an excellent lesson both for him and for you if I had. It would have taught you both better manners.

LORD GORING. Oh! bother Tommy Trafford. Tommy is a silly little ass. I love you.

MABEL CHILTERN. I know. And I think you might have mentioned it before. I am sure I have given you heaps of opportunities.

LORD GORING. Mabel, do be serious. Please be serious.

MABEL CHILTERN. Ah! that is the sort of thing a man always says to a girl before he has been married to her. He never says it afterwards.

LORD GORING (*taking hold of her hand*). Mabel, I have told you that I love you. Can't you love me a little in return?

MABEL CHILTERN. You silly Arthur! If you knew anything about . . . anything, which you don't, you would know that I adore you. Everyone in London knows it except you. It is a public scandal the way I adore you. I have been going about for the last six months telling the whole of society that I adore you. I wonder you consent to have anything to say to me. I have no character left at all. At least, I feel so happy that I am quite sure I have no character left at all.

LORD GORING (*catches her in his arms and kisses her. Then there is a pause of bliss*). Dear! Do you know I was awfully afraid of being refused!

MABEL CHILTERN (*looking up at him*). But you never have been refused yet by anybody, have you, Arthur? I can't imagine anyone refusing you.

LORD GORING (*after kissing her again*). Of course I'm not nearly good enough for you, Mabel.

MABEL CHILTERN (*nestling close to him*). I am so glad, darling. I was afraid you were.

LORD GORING (*after some hesitation*). And I'm . . . I'm a little over thirty.

MABEL CHILTERN. Dear, you look weeks younger than that.

LORD GORING (*enthusiastically*). How sweet of you to say so! . . . And it is only fair to tell you frankly that I am fearfully extravagant.

MABEL CHILTERN. But so am I, Arthur. So we're sure to agree. And now I must go and see Gertrude.

LORD GORING. Must you really?

Kisses her.

MABEL CHILTERN. Yes.

LORD GORING. Then do tell her I want to talk to her particularly. I have been waiting here all the morning to see either her or Robert.

MABEL CHILTERN. Do you mean to say you didn't come here expressly to propose to me?

LORD GORING (*triumphantly*). No; that was a flash of genius.

MABEL CHILTERN. Your first.

LORD GORING (*with determination*). My last.

MABEL CHILTERN. I am delighted to hear it. Now don't stir. I'll be back in five minutes. And don't fall into any temptations while I am away.

LORD GORING. Dear Mabel, while you are away, there are none. It makes me horribly dependent on you.

Enter LADY CHILTERN.

LADY CHILTERN. Good morning, dear! How pretty you are looking!

MABEL CHILTERN. How pale you are looking, Gertrude! It is most becoming!

LADY CHILTERN. Good morning, Lord Goring!

LORD GORING (*bowing*). Good morning, Lady Chiltern!

MABEL CHILTERN (*aside to* LORD GORING). I shall be in the conservatory, under the second palm tree on the left.

LORD GORING. Second on the left?

MABEL CHILTERN (*with a look of mock surprise*). Yes; the usual palm tree.

Blows a kiss to him, unobserved by LADY CHILTERN, *and goes out.*

LORD GORING. Lady Chiltern, I have a certain amount of very good news to tell you. Mrs Cheveley gave me up Robert's letter last night, and I burned it. Robert is safe.

LADY CHILTERN (*sinking on the sofa*). Safe! Oh! I am so glad of that. What a good friend you are to him – to us!

LORD GORING. There is only one person now that could be said to be in any danger.

LADY CHILTERN. Who is that?

LORD GORING (*sitting down beside her*). Yourself.

LADY CHILTERN. I! In danger? What do you mean?

LORD GORING. Danger is too great a word. It is a word
I should not have used. But I admit I have something to
tell you that may distress you, that terribly distresses me.
Yesterday evening you wrote me a very beautiful, womanly
letter, asking me for my help. You wrote to me as one of
your oldest friends, one of your husband's oldest friends.
Mrs Cheveley stole that letter from my rooms.

LADY CHILTERN. Well, what use is it to her? Why should she
not have it?

LORD GORING (*rising*). Lady Chiltern, I will be quite frank
with you. Mrs Cheveley puts a certain construction on that
letter and proposes to send it to your husband.

LADY CHILTERN. But what construction could she put on
it? . . . Oh! not that! not that! If I in – in trouble, and
wanting your help, trusting you, propose to come to you . . .
that you may advise me . . . assist me . . . Oh! are there
women so horrible as that . . . ? And she proposes to send it
to my husband? Tell me what happened. Tell me all that
happened.

LORD GORING. Mrs Cheveley was concealed in a room
adjoining my library, without my knowledge. I thought that
the person who was waiting in that room to see me was
yourself. Robert came in unexpectedly. A chair or
something fell in the room. He forced his way in, and he
discovered her. We had a terrible scene. I still thought it was
you. He left me in anger. At the end of everything Mrs
Cheveley got possession of your letter – she stole it, when or
how, I don't know.

LADY CHILTERN. At what hour did this happen?

LORD GORING. At half past ten. And now I propose that we
tell Robert the whole thing at once.

LADY CHILTERN (*looking at him with amazement that is almost
terror*). You want me to tell Robert that the woman you

expected was not Mrs Cheveley, but myself? That it was I whom you thought was concealed in a room in your house, at half-past ten o'clock at night? You want me to tell him that?

LORD GORING. I think it is better that he should know the exact truth.

LADY CHILTERN (*rising*). Oh, I couldn't, I couldn't!

LORD GORING: May I do it?

LADY CHILTERN. No.

LORD GORING (*gravely*). You are wrong, Lady Chiltern.

LADY CHILTERN. No. The letter must be intercepted. That is all. But how can I do it? Letters arrive for him every moment of the day. His secretaries open them and hand them to him. I dare not ask the servants to bring me his letters. It would be impossible. Oh! why don't you tell me what to do?

LORD GORING. Pray be calm, Lady Chiltern, and answer the questions I am going to put to you. You said his secretaries open his letters.

LADY CHILTERN. Yes.

LORD GORING. Who is with him today? Mr Trafford, isn't it?

LADY CHILTERN. No. Mr Montford, I think.

LORD GORING. You can trust him?

LADY CHILTERN (*with a gesture of despair*). Oh! how do I know?

LORD GORING. He would do what you asked him, wouldn't he?

LADY CHILTERN. I think so.

LORD GORING. Your letter was on pink paper. He could recognise it without reading it, couldn't he? By the colour?

LADY CHILTERN. I suppose so.

LORD GORING. Is he in the house now?

LADY CHILTERN. Yes.

LORD GORING. Then I will go and see him myself, and tell him that a certain letter, written on pink paper, is to be forwarded to Robert today, and that at all costs it must not reach him. (*Goes to the door, and opens it.*) Oh! Robert is coming upstairs with the letter in his hand. It has reached him already.

LADY CHILTERN (*with a cry of pain*). Oh! you have saved his life; what have you done with mine?

Enter SIR ROBERT CHILTERN. *He has the letter in his hand, and is reading it. He comes towards his wife, not noticing* LORD GORING's *presence.*

SIR ROBERT CHILTERN. 'I want you. I trust you. I am coming to you. Gertrude.' Oh, my love! is this true? Do you indeed trust me, and want me? If so, it was for me to come to you, not for you to write of coming to me. This letter of yours, Gertrude, makes me feel that nothing that the world may do can hurt me now. You want me, Gertrude?

LORD GORING, *unseen by* SIR ROBERT CHILTERN, *makes an imploring sign to* LADY CHILTERN *to accept the situation and* SIR ROBERT's *error.*

LADY CHILTERN. Yes.

SIR ROBERT CHILTERN. You trust me, Gertrude?

LADY CHILTERN. Yes.

SIR ROBERT CHILTERN. Ah! why did you not add you loved me?

LADY CHILTERN (*taking his hand*). Because I loved you.

LORD GORING *passes into the conservatory.*

SIR ROBERT CHILTERN (*kisses her*). Gertrude, you don't know what I feel. When Montford passed me your letter across the table – he had opened it by mistake, I suppose, without looking at the handwriting on the envelope – and I read it – oh! I did not care what disgrace or punishment was in store for me, I only thought you loved me still.

LADY CHILTERN. There is no disgrace in store for you, nor any public shame. Mrs Cheveley has handed over to Lord

Goring the document that was in her possession, and he has destroyed it.

SIR ROBERT CHILTERN. Are you sure of this, Gertrude?

LADY CHILTERN. Yes; Lord Goring has just told me.

SIR ROBERT CHILTERN. Then I am safe! Oh! What a wonderful thing to be safe! For two days I have been in terror. I am safe now. How did Arthur destroy my letter? Tell me.

LADY CHILTERN. He burned it.

SIR ROBERT CHILTERN. I wish I had seen that one sin of my youth burning to ashes. How many men there are in modern life who would like to see their past burning to white ashes before them! Is Arthur still here?

LADY CHILTERN. Yes; he is in the conservatory.

SIR ROBERT CHILTERN. I am so glad now I made that speech last night in the House, so glad. I made it thinking that public disgrace might be the result. But it has not been so.

LADY CHILTERN. Public honour has been the result

SIR ROBERT CHILTERN. I think so. I fear so, almost. For although I am safe from detection, although every proof against me is destroyed, I suppose, Gertrude . . . I suppose I should retire from public life?

He looks anxiously at his wife.

LADY CHILTERN (*eagerly*). Oh yes, Robert, you should do that. It is your duty to do that.

SIR ROBERT CHILTERN. It is much to surrender.

LADY CHILTERN. No; it will be much to gain.

SIR ROBERT CHILTERN *walks up and down the room with a troubled expression. Then comes over to his wife, and puts his hand on her shoulder.*

SIR ROBERT CHILTERN. And you would be happy living somewhere alone with me, abroad perhaps, or in the country away from London, away from public life? You would have no regrets?

LADY CHILTERN. Oh! none, Robert.

SIR ROBERT CHILTERN (*sadly*). And your ambition for me? You used to be ambitious for me.

LADY CHILTERN. Oh, my ambition! I have none now, but that we two may love each other. It was your ambition that led you astray. Let us not talk about ambition.

LORD GORING returns from the conservatory, looking very pleased with himself, and with an entirely new buttonhole that someone has made for him.

SIR ROBERT CHILTERN (*going towards him*). Arthur, I have to thank you for what you have done for me. I don't know how I can repay you.

Shakes hands with him.

LORD GORING. My dear fellow, I'll tell you at once. At the present moment, under the usual palm tree . . . I mean in the conservatory . . .

Enter MASON.

MASON. Lord Caversham.

LORD GORING. That admirable father of mine really makes a habit of turning up at the wrong moment. It is very heartless of him, very heartless indeed.

Enter LORD CAVERSHAM. MASON goes out.

LORD CAVERSHAM. Good morning, Lady Chiltern! Warmest congratulations to you, Chiltern, on your brilliant speech last night. I have just left the Prime Minister, and you are to have the vacant seat in the Cabinet.

SIR ROBERT CHILTERN (*with a look of joy and triumph*). A seat in the Cabinet?

LORD CAVERSHAM. Yes; here is the Prime Minister's letter.

Hands letter.

SIR ROBERT CHILTERN (*takes letter and reads it*). A seat in the Cabinet!

LORD CAVERSHAM. Certainly, and you well deserve it too. You have got what we want so much in political life nowadays – high character, high moral tone, high principles. (*To* LORD GORING.) Everything that you have not got, sir, and never will have.

LORD GORING. I don't like principles, father. I prefer prejudices.

SIR ROBERT CHILTERN *is on the brink of accepting the Prime Minister's offer, when he sees his wife looking at him with clear, candid eyes. He then realises that it is impossible.*

SIR ROBERT CHILTERN. I cannot accept this offer, Lord Caversham. I have made up my mind to decline it.

LORD CAVERSHAM. Decline it, sir!

SIR ROBERT CHILTERN. My intention is to retire at once from public life.

LORD CAVERSHAM (*angrily*). Decline a seat in the Cabinet, and retire from public life? Never heard such damned nonsense in the whole course of my existence. I beg your pardon, Lady Chiltern. Chiltern. I beg your pardon. (*To* LORD GORING.) Don't grin like that, sir.

LORD GORING. No, father.

LORD CAVERSHAM. Lady Chiltern, you are a sensible woman, the most sensible woman in London, the most sensible woman I know. Will you kindly prevent your husband from making such a . . . from talking such . . . Will you kindly do that, Lady Chiltern?

LADY CHILTERN. I think my husband is right in his determination, Lord Caversham. I approve of it.

LORD CAVERSHAM. You approve of it? Good heavens!

LADY CHILTERN (*taking her husband's hand*). I admire him for it. I admire him immensely for it. I have never admired him so much before. He is finer than even I thought him. (*To* SIR ROBERT CHILTERN.) You will go and write your letter to the Prime Minister now, won't you? Don't hesitate about it, Robert.

SIR ROBERT CHILTERN (*with a touch of bitterness*). I suppose I had better write it at once. Such offers are not repeated. I will ask you to excuse me for a moment, Lord Caversham.

LADY CHILTERN. I may come with you, Robert, may I not?

SIR ROBERT CHILTERN. Yes, Gertrude.

LADY CHILTERN *goes out with him.*

LORD CAVERSHAM. What is the matter with the family? Something wrong here, eh? (*Tapping his forehead.*) Idiocy? Hereditary, I suppose. Both of them, too. Wife as well as husband. Very sad. Very sad indeed! And they are not an old family. Can't understand it.

LORD GORING It is not idiocy, father, I assure you.

LORD CAVERSHAM. What is it then, sir.

LORD GORING (*after some hesitation*). Well, it is what is called nowadays a high moral tone, father. That is all.

LORD CAVERSHAM. Hate these new-fangled names. Same thing as we used to call idiocy fifty years ago. Shan't stay in this house any longer.

LORD GORING (*taking his arm*). Oh! just go in here for a moment, father. Second palm tree to the left, the usual palm tree.

LORD CAVERSHAM. What, sir?

LORD GORING. I beg your pardon, father, I forgot. The conservatory, father, the conservatory – there is someone there I want you to talk to.

LORD CAVERSHAM. What about, sir?

LORD GORING. About me, father.

LORD CAVERSHAM (*grimly*). Not a subject on which much eloquence is possible.

LORD GORING No, father; but the lady is like me. She doesn't care much for eloquence in others. She thinks it a little loud.

LORD CAVERSHAM *goes into the conservatory.* LADY CHILTERN *enters.*

LORD GORING. Lady Chiltern, why are you playing Mrs Cheveley's cards?

LADY CHILTERN (*startled*). I don't understand you.

LORD GORING. Mrs Cheveley made an attempt to ruin your husband. Either to drive him from public life, or to make him adopt a dishonourable position. From the latter tragedy you saved him. The former you are now thrusting on him. Why should you do him the wrong Mrs Cheveley tried to do and failed?

LADY CHILTERN. Lord Goring?

LORD GORING (*pulling himself together for a great effort, and showing the philosopher that underlies the dandy*). Lady Chiltern, allow me. You wrote me a letter last night in which you said you trusted me and wanted my help. Now is the moment when you really want my help, now is the time when you have got to trust me, to trust in my counsel and judgement. You love Robert. Do you want to kill his love for you? What sort of existence will he have if you rob him of the fruits of his ambition, if you take him from the splendour of a great political career, if you close the doors of public life against him, if you condemn him to sterile failure, he who was made for triumph and success? Women are not meant to judge us, but to forgive us when we need forgiveness. Pardon, not punishment, is their mission. Why should you scourge him with rods for a sin done in his youth, before he knew you, before he knew himself? A man's life is of more value than a woman's. It has larger issues, wider scope, greater ambitions. A woman's life revolves in curves of emotions. It is upon lines of intellect that a man's life progresses. Don't make any terrible mistake, Lady Chiltern. A woman who can keep a man's love, and love him in return, has done all the world wants of women, or should want of them.

LADY CHILTERN (*troubled and hesitating*). But it is my husband himself who wishes to retire from public life. He feels it is his duty. It was he who first said so.

LORD GORING. Rather than lose your love, Robert would do anything, wreck his whole career, as he is on the brink of doing now. He is making for you a terrible sacrifice. Take my advice, Lady Chiltern, and do not accept a sacrifice so great. If you do you will live to repent it bitterly. We men and women are not made to accept such sacrifices from each other. We are not worthy of them. Besides, Robert has been punished enough.

LADY CHILTERN. We have both been punished. I set him up too high.

LORD GORING (*with deep feeling in his voice*). Do not for that reason set him down now too low. If he has fallen from his altar, do not thrust him into the mire. Failure to Robert would be the very mire of shame. Power is his passion. He would lose everything, even his power to feel love. Your husband's life is at this moment in your hands, your husband's love is in your hands. Don't mar both for him.

Enter SIR ROBERT CHILTERN.

SIR ROBERT CHILTERN. Gertrude, here is the draft of my letter. Shall I read it to you?

LADY CHILTERN. Let me see it.

SIR ROBERT *hands her the letter. She reads it, and then, with a gesture of passion, tears it up.*

SIR ROBERT CHILTERN. What are you doing?

LADY CHILTERN. A man's life is of more value than a woman's. It has larger issues, wider scope, greater ambitions. Our lives revolve in curves of emotions. It is upon lines of intellect that a man's life progresses. I have just learnt this, and much else with it, from Lord Goring. And I will not spoil your life for you, nor see you spoil it as a sacrifice to me, a useless sacrifice!

SIR ROBERT CHILTERN. Gertrude! Gertrude!

LADY CHILTERN. You can forget. Men easily forget. And I forgive. That is how women help the world. I see that now.

SIR ROBERT CHILTERN (*deeply overcome by emotion, embraces her*). My wife! my wife! (*To* LORD GORING.) Arthur, it seems that I am always to be in your debt.

LORD GORING. Oh dear no, Robert. Your debt is to Lady Chiltern, not to me!

SIR ROBERT CHILTERN. I owe you much. And now tell me
what you were going to ask me just now as Lord Caversham
came in.

LORD GORING. Robert, you are your sister's guardian, and
I want your consent to my marriage with her. That is all.

LADY CHILTERN. Oh, I am so glad! I am so glad!

Shakes hands with LORD GORING.

LORD GORING. Thank you, Lady Chiltern.

SIR ROBERT CHILTERN (*with a troubled look*). My sister to be
your wife?

LORD GORING. Yes.

SIR ROBERT CHILTERN (*speaking with great firmness*). Arthur,
I am very sorry, but the thing is quite out of the question. I
have to think of Mabel's future happiness. And I don't think
her happiness would be safe in your hands. And I cannot
have her sacrificed!

LORD GORING. Sacrificed!

SIR ROBERT CHILTERN. Yes, utterly sacrificed. Loveless
marriages are horrible. But there is one thing worse than an
absolutely loveless marriage. A marriage in which there is
love, but on one side only; faith, but on one side only;
devotion, but on one side only, and in which of the two
hearts one is sure to be broken.

LORD GORING. But I love Mabel. No other woman has any
place in my life.

LADY CHILTERN. Robert, if they love each other, why should
they not be married?

SIR ROBERT CHILTERN. Arthur cannot bring Mabel the
love that she deserves.

LORD GORING. What reason have you for saying that?

SIR ROBERT CHILTERN (*after a pause*). Do you really require
me to tell you?

LORD GORING. Certainly I do.

SIR ROBERT CHILTERN. As you choose. When I called on
you yesterday evening I found Mrs Cheveley concealed in

your rooms. It was between ten and eleven o'clock at night.
I do not wish to say anything more. Your relations with Mrs
Cheveley have, as I said to you last night, nothing whatso-
ever to do with me. I know you were engaged to be married
to her once. The fascination she exercised over you then
seems to have returned. You spoke to me last night of her
as of a woman pure and stainless, a woman whom you
respected and honoured. That may be so. But I cannot give
my sister's life into your hands. It would be wrong of me.
It would be unjust, infamously unjust to her.

LORD GORING. I have nothing more to say.

LADY CHILTERN. Robert, it was not Mrs Cheveley whom
Lord Goring expected last night.

SIR ROBERT CHILTERN. Not Mrs Cheveley! Who was it
then?

LORD GORING. Lady Chiltern!

LADY CHILTERN. It was your own wife. Robert, yesterday
afternoon Lord Goring told me that if ever I was in trouble
I could come to him for help, as he was our oldest and best
friend. Later on, after that terrible scene in this room,
I wrote to him telling him that I trusted him, that I had
need of him, that I was coming to him for help and advice.
(SIR ROBERT CHILTERN *takes the letter out of his pocket.*)
Yes, that letter. I didn't go to Lord Goring's, after all. I felt
that it is from ourselves alone that help can come. Pride
made me think that. Mrs Cheveley went. She stole my letter
and sent it anonymously to you this morning, that you
should think . . . Oh! Robert, I cannot tell you what she
wished you to think . . .

SIR ROBERT CHILTERN. What! Had I fallen so low in your
eyes that you thought that even for a moment I could have
doubted your goodness? Gertrude, Gertrude, you are to me
the white image of all good things, and sin can never touch
you. Arthur, you can go to Mabel, and you have my best
wishes! Oh! stop a moment. There is no name at the beginning of this letter. The brilliant Mrs Cheveley does not seem
to have noticed that. There should be a name.

LADY CHILTERN. Let me write yours. It is you I trust and need. You and none else.

LORD GORING. Well, really, Lady Chiltern, I think I should have back my own letter.

LADY CHILTERN (*smiling*). No; you shall have Mabel. (*Takes the letter and writes her husband's name on it.*)

LORD GORING. Well, I hope she hasn't changed her mind. It's nearly twenty minutes since I saw her last.

Enter MABEL CHILTERN *and* LORD CAVERSHAM.

MABEL CHILTERN. Lord Goring, I think your father's conversation much more improving than yours. I am only going to talk to Lord Caversham in the future, and always under the usual palm tree.

LORD GORING. Darling!

Kisses her.

LORD CAVERSHAM (*considerably taken aback*). What does this mean, sir? You don't mean to say that this charming, clever young lady has been so foolish as to accept you?

LORD GORING. Certainly, father! And Chiltern's been wise enough to accept the seat in the Cabinet.

LORD CAVERSHAM. I am very glad to hear that, Chiltern . . . I congratulate you, sir. If the country doesn't go to the dogs or the Radicals, we shall have you Prime Minister, some day.

Enter MASON.

MASON. Luncheon is on the table, my Lady! (MASON *goes out.*)

MABEL CHILTERN. You'll stop to luncheon, Lord Caversham, won't you?

LORD CAVERSHAM. With pleasure, and I'll drive you down to Downing Street afterwards, Chiltern. You have a great future before you, a great future. (*To* LORD GORING.) Wish I could say the same for you, sir. But your career will have to be entirely domestic.

LORD GORING. Yes, father, I prefer it domestic.

LORD CAVERSHAM. And if you don't make this young lady an ideal husband, I'll cut you off with a shilling.

MABEL CHILTERN. An ideal husband! Oh, I don't think I should like that. It sounds like something in the next world.

LORD CAVERSHAM. What do you want him to be then, dear?

MABEL CHILTERN. He can be what he chooses. All I want is to be . . . to be . . . oh! a real wife to him.

LORD CAVERSHAM. Upon my word, there is a good deal of common sense in that, Lady Chiltern.

They all go out except SIR ROBERT CHILTERN. *He sinks into a chair, rapt in thought. After a little time* LADY CHILTERN *returns to look for him.*

LADY CHILTERN (*leaning over the back of the chair*). Aren't you coming in, Robert?

SIR ROBERT CHILTERN (*taking her hand*). Gertrude, is it love you feel for me, or is it pity merely?

LADY CHILTERN (*kisses him*). It is love, Robert. Love, and only love. For both of us a new life is beginning.

Curtain.

Glossary

a la marquise – French, in the style of a marchioness (wife or widow of a marquess – peer ranking between duke and earl).

Adam room – room constructed in the style developed by Robert Adam with his brother James in the mid-18th century. The style was primarily decorative, and the design covered every aspect, from carpets to all ornamentation.

Bath, pump room – Bath was the leading centre, outside of London, for English high society in the 18th and early 19th centuries. The pump room refers to the spa, which was a highlight when Bath was a fashionable resort.

Bimetallism – monetary standard or system based upon the use of two metals – usually gold and silver – which would automatically establish a rate of exchange between the two metals.

Blue Books – a British government publication, usually the report of a royal commission or a committee, bound in a stiff blue paper cover.

Boodle's Club – London gentleman's club.

Book of Numbers – fourth book of the Bible. Lord Goring is implying that Mrs Cheveley's marriages paralleled the sufferings outlined in the Book of Numbers.

Boucher – Francois Boucher (1703-1779) French engraver and designer, famous for sensuous and light-hearted mythical paintings and pastoral landscapes.

Canning – George Canning, (1770-1827). Spoke in the House of Commons against the theme of 'Measures not man' (1801).

Claridge's – luxury hotel in the heart of London.

Corot – Jean-Baptiste Camille Corot (1796-1875), a painter of sensual land and seascapes and of young girls and women.

décolleté – French, low neck gown.

en grêle – French, literally 'hailstones', in this context it probably means unsophisticated, having committed a *faux pas* (social error).

Factory Acts – a series of acts that were carried out to improve working conditions in factories.

Garter – highest order of English knighthood.

Higher Education for Women – political movement headed by Emily Davies, Frances Mary Buss, Henry Sidgwick, Anne Clough and other educators in the middle to late 19th century.

House of Lords – the upper chamber of British Parliament.

Inverness cape – loose belted coat having a cape with a close-fitting round collar.

Ladies' Gallery – viewing gallery overlooking the House of Commons, largely dominated by the wives of government ministers. It was eliminated by the expansion of the Parliamentary Press Gallery.

Lambeth Conference – council of Anglican bishops.

Lamia-like – image taken from Greek and Roman mythology. A lamia was a man-eating monster, characterised with a woman's head and breasts and a serpent's body. This creature was said to feed on the blood of children.

Lawrence – Sir Thomas Lawrence (1769-1830) fashionable English portrait painter of the late 18th and early 19th centuries. He often presented his models in a theatrical manner that produced romantic portraiture of a high order.

Louis Seize – French Neo-classical style which started in the 1750's. First applied to French furniture, the neo-classical style gradually replaced the curves and decorative motifs of Rococo.

Lower House – also called the House of Commons.

Moue – French, pout.

old Greek – Odysseus, a king of Ithaca and Greek leader in the Trojan War, subject of Homer's epic poem, The Odyssey, recounting Odysseus' wanderings after the war.

Panama – Panama Canal, man-made waterway linking the Pacific Ocean with the Caribbean, and created so that ships no longer had to travel via Cape Horn.

Parliamentary Franchise – the entitlement to vote in parliamentary elections.

Penelope – wife of Odysseus who waited for him during his twenty years absence.

Row – Rotten Row in Hyde Park, a popular site for promenading by the élite.

Royal Academy – society of artists, founded in 1768, under the patronage of King George III.

sang-froid – French, cold and calculated self possession.

Suez Canal – international project that was developed following the Crimean War by Ferdinand de Lesseps to link England and France to India, via Egypt.

Tanagra statuette – a terra cotta figure dating primarily from the 3rd century BC, and named after the site in Boetia in Greece.

The Morning Post – The daily newspaper that began circulation in 1772 and later merged with *The Daily Telegraph*.

Van Dyck – Sir Anthony Van Dyck (1599-1641) prominent Flemish portrait painter of European aristocracy.

voilà tout – French, roughly, 'that's it, that's the end of the story'.

Watteau – (Jean-) Antoine Watteau (1684-1721) a French painter who typified the charm and grace of the Rococo style. Much of his work reflects the influence of the Commedia dell' Arte and the Opera Ballet.

Women's Liberal Association – federation of women, whose remit was to promote the interests of the Liberal party.

Yellow book – cheap, sensational novel, notable for being bound in yellow board or paper covers. This reference underlines Mrs Cheveley's character as one who tends towards boldness and indelicacy, especially in conjunction with Lady Markby's allusion to the more formal government Blue Books.